REVIE\ SESSIO

CW01558436

Jennifer improved 100%. *"Target improvement was 30% and actual improvement was 100%! Good techniques to practice. Thanks!"*
Jennifer Bodie – Analyst – Goldman Sachs

Chrissy improved 80%. *"I can see the tangible results of the short training. Plus practice going forward, I am confident that my reading speed will be a lot faster!"*
Chrissy Cao – Auditor – KPMG

Anthony improved 113%. *"Techniques put to practice, showing tangible improvement in speed of reading. Good balance of class talk and practice."*
Anthony Schiller – Programmer – Thomson Reuters

Sandrine improved 84%. *"I could read faster while actually improving my understanding. Ideas did stick."*
Sandrine Andre – Business Analyst – J. P. Morgan

Abhijeet improved 125%. *"I did like the course. In true sense, the potential was not realised. Achieved quite a lot of understanding of different techniques and would try to improve it."*
Abhijeet Kulkami – Engineer – General Electric

Emma improved 165%. *"I think the techniques taught are very valuable and I'll be able to keep using them and improve."*
Emma Gibson – Editor – Sage

Louise improved 147%. *"Information was very well presented and was effective when put into practice. I also feel inspired to read more."*
Louise Simpkins – Risk Manager – Bank of America

Ritesh improved 70%. *"It forced us to think about our reading speed and encouraged improving this."*
Ritesh Ramji – Infrastructure Finance Adviser – PwC

Martin improved 125%. *"It was a fascinating insight into speed reading and I feel inspired to read more. I just wish I'd done this years ago. It was excellent!"*
Martin Dannhouser – Policy Advisor – Home Office

Jide improved 112%. *"Good examples, enthusiastic and love to hear more about memory skills."*
Jide Odunsi – Trader – Goldman Sachs

Alexander improved 76%. *"Made me think about the written word in a number of different ways."*
Alexander Apponyi – SVP – Brookfield Asset Management

Sherjeel improved 123%. *"Taught me about the areas I need to focus on to improve comprehension and speed."*
Sherjeel Ahmed – Vice President Finance – Barclays

Jo improved 55%. *"Great course. Very helpful. Potentially revolutionary to my life."*
Jo Evans – Sales Trading – Citigroup

Lindsey improved 86%. *"Very insightful, scientific and easy to follow."*
Lindsey Harper – Concessions Manager – Harrods

Kellie improved 213%. *"Don't know where to start. I learned much more than how to read faster. Amazing tools for life and I am inspired to be better."*

Kellie Golboume – Sales Executive – The Walt Disney Company

Thomas improved 165%. *"Liked it because I feel as I can read faster and not feel as tired when reading."*

Thomas Fonzo – Jornalist – The Wall Street Journal

Nikki improved 317%. *"I have found it extremely useful. I have struggled with reading since I was a child and I feel that these tools are good to really kick stat a new passion for reading."*

Nikki Jones – Marketing Sponsorship Executive – O2

Ahilan improved 82%. *"Very informative and useful – able to apply skills to everyday life. Very good course. Wish I had been on this course years ago."*

Ahilan Pathmanathan – Doctor – NHS

Ben improved 55%. *"Very professional and also enjoyable course (would definitely recommend to others). Good amount of knowledge learnt in a short space of time."*

Ben Sparke – Equities Trader – J. P. Morgan

Petar improved 140%. *"Great course, I definitely liked it! I learned some very useful techniques and concepts."*

Petar Lipovyanov – Analyst – HSBC

Michael improved 130%. *"Course presentation was concise and immediately relevant. Both the theory and practical aspects of course sustained my attention."*

Michael Emealo – Technical Director – Chelsea FC

Marina improved 145%. *"Variety of information presented in a very common sense way. The instructor is highly entertaining."*
Marina Potok – Manager – UBS

Andre improved 176%. *"I am happy I can read faster. Good tempo. Great presenter."*
Andre White – Relationship Manager – Lloyds Banking Group

Ellie improved 59%. *"Fantastic. Real Return on Investment! Very lovely presenter!"*
Ellie Moseley – Business Development – Thomson Reuters

Flora improved 63%. *"I wish speed reading courses could be made compulsory at every law school and university. I can't believe learning a few simple reading techniques could have saved me half the anxiety of exams and standardised tests not to mention thousands of pounds spent on testing materials and some law courses. I'd say it is one of the most rewarding amounts I've spent on my career! Definitely worth the money."*
Flora Mutuku – Law student – BPP Law School

Tom improved 243%. *"Excellent, interesting, quantifiable results in a very short period of time, value for money, clearly a well oiled machine that seemed to work for all that attended!"*
Tom Mc Grath – Project Manager – RBS GBM

Rajit improved 83%. *"Alex is a very engaging speaker. This presentation is well honed, practiced and very, very well executed."*
Rajit Singh – Software Engineer – eBay

TIME TO READ THIS BOOK

(wpm = words per minute)

SPEED	TIME
at 100 wpm	7.6 hr
at 200 wpm	3.8 hr
at 300 wpm	2.5 hr
at 400 wpm	1.9 hr
at 500 wpm	1.5 hr
at 600 wpm	1.3 hr
at 700 wpm	1.1 hr
at 800 wpm	57 min
at 900 wpm	51 min
at 1000 wpm	46 min

 **SKIP THE INTRO** ™

To skip the introduction and jump straight into the action, go to page 45. You can always read about the reason why I wrote this book after finishing it.

I believe that you will be reading faster before you reach the end of the third chapter. And even if you skip passages you don't connect with, you will still find what you are looking for.

To your success,

ALEX GARCEZ

READ 50%
FASTER TODAY

Even if English isn't your first language, you
will read 50%+ faster by the end of this book.
I guarantee your success or your money back!

ALEX GARCEZ

MIND'S EYE PRESS
Mind's Eye Press is incorporated as
Mind's Eye Training Ltd Reg. No. 08159615
Address and contact details can be found at
www.thespeedreadingcoach.com

First Edition published in Great Britain in 2017
By Mind's Eye Press

A CIP catalogue record for this book is available
from the British Library.

Disclaimer.

This book is not intended to teach you how to read, but to question the
way you read in order to increase your reading performance.

I've tested many products and services that can be helpful to you, and
I recommend the best ones throughout the book. I might receive a
commission from some of them, so I advise you to make your own
research before deciding about any purchase. I don't take any
responsibility for third party products and services.

Cover layout, illustrations and photographs © Alex Garcez

Alex' photographs by John Cassidy - www.theheadshotguy.co.uk

ISBN 978-0-9932190-5-4

To beautiful Lollie for opening my heart to love.

To my Mother and Father. Thank you for
awakening my interest in learning.

CONTRIBUTING TO A PEACEFUL WORLD WITH WEALTHY CITIZENS

I believe that ignorance generates violence, so my way of contributing to a peaceful world is by teaching people how to read faster, so they can develop their passion for reading books and for learning.

I'm confident that by reading more books you will become wealthier. *"According to the U.S. Labor Department, business people who read at least seven business books per year earn over 230 percent more than people who read just one book per year."* [1]

So, how about that for a challenge?

GUARANTEE

I'm committed to delivering results, so if you read the entire book and don't think it helped you increase your reading performance by 50%, you can send it to me with proof of purchase and I will refund the money paid, if you bought a brand new paper copy of the book. To receive a refund of an eBook you should forward the email with proof of purchase to me and also attach a picture with you holding the eBook open on Chapter 5. I will refund the money paid if your face is visible and the book content is readable on the picture. The guarantee expires 30 days after purchase. Requests for refund made 30 days after the invoice date will not be valid for a refund. You can find my address and email address at www.thespeedreadingcoach.com.

If you feel that your potential has not been realised, please send me an email with your feedback, and tell me about your needs and expectations. I'm more than happy to help you develop yourself further.

FAIR EXCHANGE

In the event that you get more value from my book than the amount you have paid, I invite you to buy one or more copies of this book and give them as a gift to people you care about, so they will develop their passion for reading books and progress in their careers at speed.

You can also donate money to my cause, and help young people and adults who struggle with the written word or who don't read for pleasure.
Can you imagine not being able to read well?

One in six adults in the UK struggles to read and they find it difficult to develop themselves.

Did you know that reading for pleasure is more important to children's successes than education or social class?

I'm supporting The Reading Agency's initiative to make English pupils the most literate in Europe within five years. I share their enthusiasm, and I am dedicated to helping them achieve this goal faster.

You can do the same!

THE
READING
AGENCY

The Reading Agency inspires more people to read more, encourage them to share their enjoyment of reading and celebrate the difference that reading makes to all our lives. Because everything changes when we read.

Learn more and make a donation at:

www.thespeedreadingcoach.com/donate

CONTENTS

Chapter 3

Part 1: Achieve good comprehension

Part 2: Reading really fast

Part 3: Understand how to see more

Part 4: Developing flexibility

Part 5: Bounce around and be in charge

Part 6: Breaking an old habit

Part 7: Saying the keywords and remembering them

LEADING THE
READING REVOLUTION

We can go deeper into any area of knowledge to incredible levels of abstraction, but one common denominator that unites all human knowledge, is that it has been written down into words and therefore, we must read to learn anything in depth.

What is surprising is that we learn how to read at five or six years of age, and then once we can read out loud – and at a good pace – our parents and teachers think that we have achieved what was expected from us. As teenagers, we have the ability to read at a level of speed that – for most of us – we will maintain for the rest of our lives.

Modernising literacy is long overdue

There is an ongoing debate about the best approach to teach reading. There are two main schools of thought. Synthetic phonics involves teaching the alphabet and then teaching children to read words, while analytic phonics teaches reading using flash cards with whole words and pictures depicting the meanings of the words.

The English language is very complex to learn because words are pronounced differently from how they are written. Synthetic phonics teaches children the sound of letters and then expects them to learn how to write the words correctly. This is not a good method because words do not sound as they are written. Teaching a strategy that has many exceptions to the rule can cause confusion, could contribute to the development of dyslexia, can cause spelling mistakes and can ultimately result in children feeling insecure in their ability to express their thoughts in writing.

I believe children should be encouraged to keep learning how to read using the whole-word approach or analytic phonics, even if they already know the alphabet.

To be able to read faster, you need to see whole words instead of trying to connect all the individual letters every time you read a word. If you teach children using analytic phonics, they will learn how to read words as if they are pictures or icons. They will naturally read faster and will be able to read aloud at a good pace. If they learn the principles described in the next chapters, they will ultimately be able to speed read.

Approaching the point of astonishingly fast change

We are living in exponential times, and we need to develop our reading skills to be able to thrive in this competitive world.

Have you heard of the Singularity University and the X Prize?

These organisations are creating the future, faster than traditional institutions, by promoting innovation that helps solve the grand challenges of our times; Google them to be surprised.

One simple premise that predicts extraordinary breakthroughs in all sciences is the *Law of Accelerating Returns*. As we now use computers in virtually every area of life, instead of developing linearly over the next 30 years, we will be developing exponentially. This is hard to imagine, so let me give you an example:

We are used to linear thinking - if I give you one penny every single day, by the end of the month, you will have 30 pennies. Now, if you think exponentially, I will give you one penny on the first day of the month and will double the amount every single day. You will be surprised to know that, by the end of the month, you will have £5,368,709.12 instead of £0.30. Yes, it is incredible that one single penny can become five million pounds in just 30 days.

Similarly, Information Technology basically doubles in power every year. Conversely, your laptop could be 536,870,912 times more powerful in 30 years time. Most fields of knowledge and sciences use IT and will also develop at a fantastic pace. As a result, you will have to learn huge amounts to make an impact within your area of work.

Don't you think that now is the right time to start improving the way you read?

Reading 50% faster will make a massive difference to your professional life, but what about being able to become more selective while focusing your attention? You could easily 2X or 5X your reading performance.

We have been taught how to read in the same linear way for hundreds of years, and I believe that it is about time to question and improve our learning skills and as well as our books. I'm developing a new way to convey information and will be publishing the books of the future very soon. Please get in touch if you want to contribute to this project.

Expected results from reading this book

After taking a 4 hour session with me (or reading this book), you can still read at the speed you used to read before the training; however, your comprehension will have improved because you will have understood certain principles that will help you to find the important information in any text.

To illustrate, let's talk about Joe, an example of a typical adult, who speaks at 250 words per minute. While reading, his comprehension is best if he reads around 250 words per minute, too.

If Joe pushes to go faster, he can go up to 300 words per minute, but his comprehension will suffer a little. If he goes faster than that, his understanding of the text will plummet to very low levels.

At 400 he is skimming the text and hardly learns anything from it. He can scan the text at around 500 words per minute and find a specific word or expression.

After a 4 hour session, instead of skimming at 400 words per minute, Joe will be reading at this speed with a good level of attention and understanding. Joe's reading speed picks up at 400 words per minute instead of 250 words per minute. On average, Joe has improved by 60%.

By observing the graph on the next page, you can see how Joe can get more from the text at 400 than at 250 words per minute.

Like Joe, most people read at the same speed they talk, therefore similar results can be achieved by reading this book.

Joe's comprehension and reading speed
before and after a 4 hour session

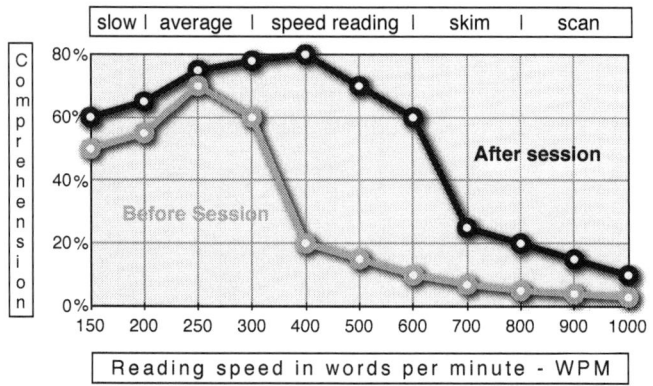

Before a 4 hour session - comprehension peaks at 250 WPM

After a 4 hour session - comprehension peaks at 400 WPM

Even if you think that you read quickly, you can improve your ability even further.

Wherever you are is a good place to start

I can guarantee that by reading this book, your reading speed will improve by 50% or I will give you your money back (brand new paper copy or eBook). I believe that you can achieve it, which is why I can ensure success.

While reading this book you will gain insights, which will automatically take you out of your comfort zone.

Speed reading bridges the gap between reading and scanning by boosting comprehension.

You may be lucky enough to read faster than your peers, yet you probably can't explain to anyone else how to read faster.

The harsh reality is that you are on your own to develop this essential skill.

This is a real disaster. Any skill can be improved with further training, and reading is no different.

So, why is almost no one teaching young kids and adults to read faster? Perhaps because they don't know how to teach this subject matter. Or is it because most people simply do not acquire this knowledge? How odd!

I am here to lead a revolution and help everyone read faster and more efficiently. It starts with a simple test that you can do at home. You can measure your reading speed in words per minute. Just time yourself to read for one minute and count the number of words you read in that time. This way you will know how fast you read and will be able to start improving your speed and comprehension levels.

Humans are obsessed with measuring everything. We know the speed of light, the rpm of an airplane engine and the frequency that your brain works in cycles per second. So why does no one talk about measuring the speed that we read?

I have launched *The Read 50% Faster Challenge* to make everyone aware of how fast they read and I am setting new standards of reading speed. I know for a fact that you can improve your reading speed and this way, you will be more likely to grab a book to read in your spare time and have fun with it!

Reading at work

I believe that the success of a company is directly proportionate to the ability of a team to process information at speed so they can solve problems, promote innovation and increase productivity.

The good news is that I have discovered that the brain actually loves speed.

I think that fast is fun – slow is boring! If you think you have a short attention span when reading books, documents and emails, then you probably read slowly and carefully. Instead of understanding the text you get bored and distracted. The main reason for this is that your brain is too powerful to go at such a slow pace and will drift off into something more interesting to think about.

You may be measuring productivity output of your team, but what about their productivity input?

How fast are they taking information in?

Reading is essential in business. The amount of information available to us is doubling every year and information is getting out of date faster than ever. By learning how to read faster and smarter you will be more focused; your mind will stop wandering and you will have better comprehension of any text. The result is that you will achieve peak performance the easy way and will become more productive.

Understand why your brain actually loves speed by reading this book. Watch the short videos I recommend and practise the techniques by reading your own books. You will develop to such levels, you would never have thought possible.

I assure you that you are a genius so, go on, read the book and apply your wisdom. You will be surprised with your hidden potential.

And please get in touch if you need any extra support. I am more than happy to help you develop and learn about your mysterious and magical mind.

HOW I SHIFTED
MY MIND

It all started with my own frustration with reading. I found it hard to keep up and was much slower than my parents, friends and peers.

Learning to cheat

As a teenager, I would try to pay attention at school, so I would not have to study at home. Back then, I felt afraid of books and inadequate but I developed coping mechanisms, and managed to finish my basic education in Brazil. Even though I would study hard, I confess that, out of desperation, I had to deal with the moral dilemma of whether to cheat during my exams or not. After weeks of anxiety, I made my decision; I was ready to cheat. I developed a sophisticated way to cheat by writing information on the surface of a translucent BIC pen with a needle. I could fit three lines of text on each side; my grades improved.

I was 17 when I had to decide my future by choosing which university degree to take. My grandfather was the chancellor of one of the most prestigious Agriculture universities in Brazil, and my uncle had just won a medal from the Brazilian president as his farm was considered to be the best modern farm in the country. I loved my holidays at the farm, and always had fun with horses, so I thought that becoming a farmer was meant to be my destiny and enrolled.

Cheating death to wake up

It is June 1986, and the end of term is approaching quickly. I am petrified because I've stopped attending classes a month earlier without telling my dad. While trying to figure out what to do next, I start hanging out with other dropouts. At first, I felt relief and inspired to find a new direction in life, but as the days passed I found myself drinking during the day and becoming insecure and depressed.

Driving back home after a sad party was when I had my wake up call. While drunk, I looked at the red lights at the bottom of a hill and dared to cross them. Yes, I had lost my mind. I was alone in the car daring myself to do something really stupid.

As I approach the point of no return at 80 miles per hour, I see a blue car zooming in front of me, then I'm almost inside the junction box and a white car crosses in front of me like a dart.

As I look to the right, I can see the headlights of a big car approaching really fast. I merged with the lights and couldn't look away, but suddenly the connection was broken and I was thrown back into reality.

I never felt more alive in my life and I had to stop the car to catch my breath. Cheating death made me go from drunk to sober in a millisecond and at that moment I realised that I had to face my fears.

Facing my fears

My father was a serious man who worked as a Bank director during the day and as a teacher of Economics at a reputable university at night. The heavy frame of his bifocals made him look intimidating and all of my friends were afraid of him. In fact, they gave him the sweet nickname of "Thunder Voice".

We had a library room at my house, and he would spend most of his free time there, reading. I approached him and asked sheepishly:

"Dad? Can we talk?"

He looked at me in dismay and said:

"Wait a moment."

He made me wait for a couple of minutes standing in front of him, while he finished reading an article in the paper.

31

Every second seemed to drag forever, and I started to sweat, as I was getting even more nervous. Finally, he looked at me and asked.

"What is the matter?"

"I've got a big problem. I've failed a few subjects at the university, even though I've studied hard, so I think I'm not cut out for it.

I want to open a shop to sell home appliances and I can also fix them if I have a workshop at the back of the shop. I am sure I can make good money if you help me get started. Would you like to become my business partner?"

He looked at me intrigued and didn't get angry, as I was expecting.

Instead, he stood up slowly and started browsing his books. He selected three books and handed them to me, while staring at me with compassion, and said:

"Read these business books. We will talk again after you have read them. If you want a business, you will have to take a Business degree."

I took the books and disappeared from his sight as quickly as I could. I was happy that I was brave enough to tell him about my ambitions, but I realised that books would be in my life forever, even if all I wanted was to become an entrepreneur and have a little shop.

Finding hope in an unsuspected place

My friend Cid could read a book overnight, so I went to see him for advice.

"Cid, I'm in a pickle and I need your help. I gave up my degree and I want to become a business man. The problem is that my dad wants me to take a Business degree. I think he will support me but he told me to read three business books before we talk again. Can you read the books and explain to me what are they about? I simply can't focus with all the stress."

He smiled and said:

"Alex, let's go for a ride."

Cid invited me to get inside of his beautiful convertible and told me that he wanted to show me something amazing. We were having fun until I saw the university gates approaching. He stopped the car and we went inside the main building. He suddenly stopped in front of one of the notice boards, looked at me and said:

"This is the solution for your life."

I was looking at posters advertising dancing classes, a chess tournament, a talk about human rights, a garage band competition and a few other events, but I couldn't find the solution for my life there. I looked back at him puzzled, so he said:

"Can't you see that there is a speed reading demonstration on Thursday?"

"No, I don't."

I couldn't see it, just inches away from my nose.

I had disconnected with studying and for this reason I was blind to the speed reading ad.

While I was a little disappointed that I had to spend the money saved for my holidays on the course, I did it anyway. But I was excited to finally understand how successful readers read, and I knew I would not be the same after the course.

A new world of possibilities

It was money well spent because I discovered that I could actually read faster than before and, to my surprise, I started enjoying my father's business books; so much so that I started going to the university's library to read marketing books, just for fun. I was hooked and, without wasting any more time, started a Business Studies degree.

Soon after taking this speed reading course, I realised I was not struggling on my own. My friend, Marcelo, had a brother that was becoming very successful working at the Stock Exchange, and while having a conversation with him, he opened up and said he didn't know how to go through all the information he had to read for work.

That was my opportunity to teach him some of what I had learnt and, for a fair payment, I had a happy client. I was on my way to starting to help people to develop their potential and perform better at reading.

Not only was I able to complete a Business Study degree, but I then went on to complete a Masters in Marketing and Advertising.

After many years of learning, researching and subsequently teaching how to focus the mind, I discovered I was dyslexic with the additional challenge of suffering from Attention Deficit Disorder (ADD).

Moving to Europe

In a quest to expand my horizons, in 1999 I moved from Brazil to London.

At first, I struggled to communicate in English, but managed to get a job in the kitchen of a Thai restaurant. Unfortunately, my co-workers spoke Thai all day long, so I resorted to learning English at night with a book and tapes, but with little motivation.

I discovered London's night life and, despite having some fun, felt lost and lonely in the big city. Without many friends I was craving to belong to a community that would help me grow as a person. I knew that in London you could pretty much find whatever you wanted, but in those pre-Google days, who could you turn to?

I made a friend at a meditation course, who invited me to a meeting to learn about personal growth. At a beautiful hotel in London, I got a foretaste of Tony Robbins. The personal development meeting was run by the Yes Group www.yesgroup.org that my friend Karl Pearsall had been inspired to create after a Tony Robbins workshop in 1993.

At the Yes Group event someone offered me a ticket for the iconic Tony Robbins workshop, Unleash The Power Within, and I bought it without hesitation. It is a four-day workshop that ends with a fire-walk. That's right. You get so pumped up that you walk on red-hot coals with a smile on your face. When you get to the other side and look back at the glowing embers, you feel like you can move mountains.

In that workshop Tony took my mind for a ride through the realm of possibilities. I was surprised to hear him recommending that everyone take a speed reading course to improve themselves. But he didn't offer to teach us, nor did he recommend a teacher. I felt that he was talking directly to me, so I decided there and then to master the English language and teach speed reading in the UK. Some of my friends scoffed at my ambitions, but I found the means to pay for English lessons at the best and most expensive course in the capital.

Once I had mastered speed reading, the seminar promoters that take Tony Robbins and other first-class speakers around the world, Success Resources www.srglobal.com, invited me to attend a Gerry Robert presentation. Gerry is a renowned expert who helps people write and publish their book — fast. Ever since I had attended Tony's event, I had dreamt of being published and Gerry explained to me how to make my book a reality. I wasted no time, started developing my own speed reading methodology and my book started taking shape.

Making a dent in the Universe

With my book proof in hand, I attended another Tony Robbins event, but this time I was determined to talk to him and invite him to become my business partner. I could see it all in my mind's eye: I would give his books to my students to practice reading faster and he would promote my speed reading workshops so people could develop themselves. A perfect partnership!

At the event I asked a lot of people to help me meet Tony, but the answer was always the same, *"No. No. No"*. I hoped that my friend Harry Singha, who was the MC of the event, would help me out, but he said, *"No-one talks to Tony privately, sorry Alex"*. That was a blow, so I went to the event's lobby to decide my next move; after a short while a woman called Lydia approached me and we started talking. She told me she was pre-launching a platform that will revolutionise education throughout the world. As I already knew the education system moves too slowly, I doubled my attention when she said that we need to prepare our youth to find or create their own jobs. I agreed that the world is moving fast and everyone should be able to learn something practical and start earning good money, even without a degree. She then introduced me to the NewTycoon platform and I joined it on the spot.

I understand that in this ever-changing world, the power of anticipation is key to success. Having first-hand information about something that is going to become huge is giving me a major advantage; I want to pass that advantage on to you, to help you propel your business faster in the unchartered waters of the future.

I knew I was on the right track but what happened next was just mind blowing. A few minutes later, Lydia introduced me to the founder of the NewTycoon platform, also the CEO of Success Resources, Richard Tan.

We started talking and laughing; he wanted to know more about my courses and I gave him the best answers and references. I was already having a great time and then he told me that he needed me to speak from the big stage at National Achievers Congress events all over the world. He said that Tony Robbins keeps advertising speed reading and that he had finally found the person he was looking for. I was speechless - a nod of my head and a smile were enough to seal the deal. I was over the moon, but that was just the beginning of the adventure.

I didn't know at the time that Success Resources is the biggest seminar promoter in the world, organising 500 events a year in 30 countries.

Richard decided to introduce me Tony Robbins because the synergy was there. Then, suddenly, against all the odds, moments later I was in front of Tony Robbins, inviting him to become my business partner, just like in my dream!

I now met Tony twice and I thank him for the initial spark that gave me the confidence to try the impossible.

Alex Garcez with Tony Robbins and Richard Tan

Since then, however, my life has taken yet another turn.

Richard Tan shared with me that NewTycoon is his biggest idea to date; the platform is using cutting-edge technology and groundbreaking content. He wants to revolutionise education and has invited me to lead the NewTycoon platform in the UK alongside two great leaders, Krishna Gurung and Harry Sardinas. I humbly accepted the mission bestowed on me and am now leading a group of motivated people who are changing the world through education, making me a global influencer.

I've always wanted to modernise the education system by showing people a better way to read and learn, and now I have found the platform from which I will be able to do it.

I was also fascinated to learn that Success Resources and NewTycoon are pioneering the use of holographic technology to project a fully formed 3D presenter on stage by partnering up with ARHT

Media. They already had Tony Robbins presenting a workshop in Melbourne, Australia to an audience, but to everyone's surprise, Tony was not there, he was actually being streamed from Miami, Florida in real time and no one could tell the difference between the real Tony or his virtual reality projection. By the way, all of it happened without the need for wearing any special glasses.

Another innovative technology that is taking the world by storm is Virtual Reality. Tony Robbins is a partner of NextVR and they are streaming one sports or music event a week in virtual reality. At the beginning of 2017 there were 10 million people with a VR headset and by the end of the year it is predicted that there will be 100 million. So, do you want to be one of the first people to experience and to create content for this new media?

I had the privilege of spending four days with Richard Tan in Bali in March 2017 and I can assure you that there is much more happening at the NewTycoon headquarters. I am convinced that NewTycoon is the future of learning.

If you want to succeed in this hyper-competitive world, share your message as a presenter or learn essential skills that schools and universities are failing to deliver, please check out NewTycoon because today might be your lucky day.

41

www.thespeedreadingcoach.com/newtycoon

Updating the education system

A lot of effort is made to teach young people to read and most teachers believe that if you can read silently at the same speed that you talk, then you can read proficiently.

This is a real shame because your brain loves speed and reading slowly can leave you disengaged and much less motivated to read in your leisure time.

A research run by The Jenkins Group in the USA shows that 42% of college graduates never read another book after college.

If you read slowly and keep skipping back to re-read you end up getting bored, and no one wants to get bored by choice, so they are wise enough to stop reading books or long texts.

Most of us read at the same speed we talk. Have you noticed that little voice inside your head repeating everything back to you? If you don't feel the need to say all the words inside your head you are not limited to read at the same speed as you talk.

My coaching career

I have personally taught more than 3,600 people and with my new method, more than 97.4% of my clients improved their reading performance by at least 33% after one session, which is a massive productivity booster. In fact, after nine years of experience I can say that most people can increase their performance by more than 100%.

I like working with clever minds; I have taught a lot of people including professionals from many high profile companies. But when I ask them if they are slow or fast readers, their response is usually vague. In fact, most suggest that they are not very fast and often compare themselves to someone else who can read material faster than they can.

You also know someone that reads faster than you, don't you? Don't worry - everybody does.

In my view, reading faster is as easy as learning to play a new video game. You might improve 33%, 50% or even more than 100% in a matter of a few hours.

Change your life

Reading faster is a natural ability that you have and, by developing it, you will be more willing to study, research and also read more books for pleasure.

I believe you can change this world in ways never thought of before. Education is a powerful way to help people innovate, improve the quality of life on our planet and promote peace in every country.

Be curious and do what you love. The possibilities are endless. Being able to learn to read faster will help you progress in life at a higher speed, plus, help you connect with so many amazing people on this planet that have a message to share inside a book.

Through action, change can happen, and through passionate action you can create flow, lead teams and leave a legacy.

The whole world is powered by imagination and the future is brighter for those who dare to dream.

HORSE & SHARK
METHOD™

The **Horse & Shark Method** provides a framework to guide you through the practical exercises. The method is made up of two systems.

The first system is the **Read Horse System**, and it will show you a smooth and simple way to read faster. Once you are confident with reading faster you will be introduced to the **Think Shark System** to develop a wider strategy to become a leading expert fast.

Watch the short videos I recommend, and use this book or other books of your choice, to practise these simple and effective techniques.

One of the most important things to do is to keep track of your progress by measuring your reading speed as you go through a book – you will see your improvement over time.

Soon you will enter a new comfort zone and will be impressed at how much faster you are reading.

A smooth and simple way to read faster.

The **Read Horse System** will show you the four steps to help improve your reading skills by showing you how to:

R   **Read** faster without training

E   **Experience** four rhythms to read

A   **Achieve** good comprehension

D   **Develop** your passion for books

To illustrate the process, I will compare the act of fast reading to learning how to ride a horse. Once you understand the process, you will be ready for the experience.

1 - Read faster without training

Can you imagine riding a beautiful horse in a 3D virtual environment? That's what you are going to do to get started.

You watch the horse approaching through your 3D glasses, then you jump into the saddle, and the mechanical horse starts moving. You feel the fresh breeze on your face as you gather speed, racing over vast green fields. As you direct the horse towards the woods, you jump over a log, and you feel exhilarated - you feel like you are riding a real horse. There will be more surprises on your journey!

I will show you how to read using simulation software, and you will start reading faster as if by magic. The words will rush towards you, and you will understand the text at an astonishingly fast pace. In this way, you will be ready to start speed reading books too.

2 - Experience four rhythms to read

If you are familiar with horses like me, you already know that all horses have four basic gaits.

They can walk at 4 mph (miles per hour), trot at 10 mph, canter at 14 mph and gallop at 30 mph. As they go faster, their legs move in specific ways.

When they trot they lift each diagonal pair of legs alternately. When they gallop all their hooves are off the ground at the same time during each stride.

In the same way, you will increase your reading speed if you understand the natural reading speed paces that suit your reading needs.

3 - Achieve good comprehension

When riding, whenever you increase your pace, you will be unstable in the saddle until you learn how to move your body in synchronisation with the horse.

When reading, your comprehension could also be wobbly when you introduce a new pace. As you get used to reading at a faster pace, you relax and start to feel confident. Once you start reading at a consistent and stable pace, your comprehension level will rise.

4 - Develop your passion for books

Some people are afraid of riding horses because they do not have the skills required to be in charge of the horse. Instead, they jump on the horse, hold on tight and let someone else pull the horse along. They think they are riding it, but they are not.

After learning how to read at different speeds, you will feel the difference between riding on a path in the woods, on the seashore or crossing a stream.

Horses like a rider who know where they are going, and gives clear directions when to turn or to increase speed.

In the same way, a marketing book will require a different set of reading speeds than a science fiction book. Instead of reading everything at one steady pace, you will be able to shift gears to speed up when you can and slow down when you need to.

Many people look at a book and think based on experience, that it would take one or two months to finish it. At the final step, you will learn how to work out the time required to read a book at your new reading speed, and will be surprised that a 200-page book might take you as little as two, three or four hours to read. You will also learn how to set up your reading targets to stay motivated to read more books, just for fun.

PART 1 - READ FASTER WITHOUT TRAINING

"In times of change, learners inherit the earth, while the learned find themselves beautifully equipped to deal with a world that no longer exists."

Eric Hoffer

By reading this chapter you can expect to improve your reading speed on a computer screen from 10–100%+. No kidding!

Time to read this chapter

at 100 wpm	38 min
at 200 wpm	19 min
at 300 wpm	13 min
at 400 wpm	9 min
at 500 wpm	8 min
at 600 wpm	6 min
at 700 wpm	5 min
at 800 wpm	5 min
at 900 wpm	4 min
at 1000 wpm	4 min

1.1.1 How fast do you read?

You may think that you read slowly or perhaps you think you are an average reader, but how do you know? Who would you compare yourself with? There are no set standards. You probably learnt to read as a child in the traditional way. There might be occasions when you get bored and distracted, read a few paragraphs, and then skip back to re-read a paragraph that you can't quite remember reading or didn't understand. Does that sound familiar? My experience suggests that most people spend one third of the time skipping back and re-reading something they've read before; this is a waste, and therefore I will help you get more focused.

The benefits of reading faster

Once you have learnt to speed read you will be more focused and your comprehension will be enhanced.

These techniques are very easy to master; however, it is essential that you follow the instructions as they are, even if at first they seem a little awkward while you practise.

By the end of this book you will be surprised by your overall performance. By following the easy-to-follow exercises on our website, you will acquire a skill for life and will therefore, become more flexible in your approach so you can speed up your reading whenever you feel that it is appropriate to do so.

Your expectations and real life

I have provided a space below so that you can write down your expectations of improvement after reading the book and practising the basic exercises. What do you think you will achieve in terms of improvement?

Will you improve 10%, 20%, 30%, 50%, 100% or more than 100%?

Because we spend so much time reading throughout each day, I believe that even a 20% improvement would save valuable time. You could be saving in excess of two or three years of your life if you spend much of your time reading.

There is no right or wrong, just have a guess. How much do you think you will improve?

Write it down here or make a note in your diary.

I expect to improve: __*100*____ %

You can get back to it at the end of the book and you will be surprised by the results.

You should aim to improve by 100%. If you set this as your target you will be more open to achieving a big change in your reading performance. Most people that take *The Read 50% Faster Challenge* with me improve by 100% or more. If you aim to improve by only 20%, you may be expecting me to prove to you that you can speed read; however, the only person that can really make it happen is you, so be ready to get more confident and increase your brain power.

Read a book like you are watching a movie

Can you imagine choosing a book to read, yet reading it as if you were watching a movie? I will show you how to read a book of approximately 200 pages in two to three hours in a motivating way.

If you are choosing a DVD to watch, you peruse the back cover to see what the movie is about, the actors, the plot and, perhaps, the running time.

Let's say that the length of the movie you've chosen to watch is one hour and 55 minutes. Although we don't always think about this, it can be reassuring to know how long it will take to watch the entire movie. On the other hand, if you were to pick up a book, it is likely that you will have no concept of how long it will take to read it. In the back of your mind you may know that you read four books the previous year, so that it takes on average three months to read a book – which is demotivating, especially if the book is "thick".

I will show you how to improve your reading speed and to understand the speed at which you are reading, so you will know beforehand how long it will take to read a book of any size.

There is no miracle and I don't exaggerate what is possible.

Learn new tricks, practise the exercises, and then you will be surprised to learn that reading a book in two or three hours is really possible.

Getting your reading speed above average

Reading in the traditional way is considered to be slow reading. We live in a fast-paced society and if you slow down to read, you will easily get bored and distracted. And you're likely to lack motivation to read, whether it's for study, work or pleasure.

People talk on average at speeds that range from 150–250 words per minute (WPM). You can see from the graph on the next page that this is the same speed at which most people read.

Based on my own experiences, I estimate that, on average, children tend to read at 150 WPM, teens at 250 WPM, rising to 300 WPM for students at university; however, after finishing their degree, most adults probably slow down to about 200 WPM. Most of the high-level executives I've worked with had an initial reading speed of around 400 WPM, while in the general population you would find one in 100 adults that read at more than 700 WPM.

What's important to understand is that everyone can boost their reading speed. It doesn't matter which category you're in.

Average reading speed, according to age and occupation, in WPM.

Reading speed in WPM (words per minute)

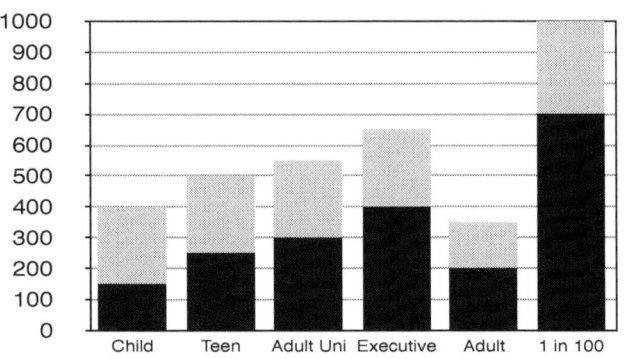

Expected improvement after reading the book
Reading speed before learning with the book

Based on more than nine years' experience of teaching people how to read faster, I believe that the younger you learn, the more significant the improvement.

Many of us can learn to read at 400-700 WPM. At this pace you might think that the voice inside your head will be going at the rate of a horse racing commentator. In fact, what happens is that you start to go faster and the voice inside your head starts to disappear, until you become a silent reader.

1.1.2 Test yourself – measure your reading speed

First of all I want to show you something very interesting. I will show you how to measure your reading speed so you can see the amazing improvement every time you measure it by yourself.

This simple test will really open your mind. This is the beginning of your training. Let's set your standards.

After the test you will be able to speed read by using amazing software.

You will achieve better results if you measure your reading speed twice, on two different books (you can use a paper book, Kindle, iPad or tablet). Your reading speed can vary quite a bit when you read different subjects, so I want you to see the difference. I will also ask you to rate your comprehension of what you've just read.

First of all you need to choose the right kind of books to make the most of the training.

Your books should be:

- Non-fiction books that you want to learn something from

- Easy read book, nothing complex to start with

- Books with an average of 10 words per line (9 or 11 words per line is still OK)

- Books with continuous text. Avoid books with many bullet points

Non-fiction books are best to learn how to speed read. After you get the hang of it, you will be able to speed read your fiction books, articles, emails and tweets too.

I will guide you through the process while you watch a short video. I will give you exactly one minute to read your book and you will find out your reading speed in words per minute (WPM). You can also use the timer on your phone to measure your reading speed.

When your minute expires, you can stop and mark the line you read. Think about what you've just read to rate your comprehension level from 1 to 10.

To help you do this through the training programme, ask yourself: Did I follow the author's train of thought? Do I remember any details from the text?

According to the answers that you give, rate your level of comprehension and then keep track of the results on your control sheet.

Next, count the number of lines you read and then multiply by the average number of words in one line. To make things simple, we will work with averages and round the numbers down. To find the average number, count the number of words in three full lines and then divide the result by three. You can then round the result down.

For example, let's say that you read 22 lines and each line has on average 10 words per line. Multiply one by the other and you will find that you are reading at 220 WPM. Next, go to the control sheet on the following page and write down the results. It is good to have a record of where you started.

Go now to the website below and I will guide you through the process.

www.thespeedreadingcoach.com/test

If you test yourself twice and keep track of the results on the control sheet you will be helping yourself to see where you currently are and then be able to improve your reading performance even further.

ALEX GARCEZ

Keeping track of your progress

Great! Now that you know your reading speed please jot it down on the appropriate boxes for "Test 1" and "Test 2" or in your diary.

CONTROL SHEET

Test 1 Baseline	Reading speed WPM	131	Reading speed increase in %
	Comprehension 1-10	5	
Test 2 Baseline	Reading speed WPM	341	
	Comprehension 1-10	7	
Fastest Zap	Reading speed WPM		%
	Comprehension 1-10		
Fastest Metro	Reading speed WPM		%
	Comprehension 1-10		
Test 3	Reading speed WPM		%
	Comprehension 1-10		
Test 4	Reading speed WPM		%
	Comprehension 1-10		
Test 5	Reading speed WPM		%
	Comprehension 1-10		
Test 6	Reading speed WPM		%
	Comprehension 1-10		

* WPM (words per minute)

This is what the results mean

Most people read at the same speed they talk; so if you talk fast, you probably read faster than those who talk slowly.

On average, adults read from 150–250 WPM.

Below is a guide to show you where you are now.

If your reading speed is:

• Below 200 WPM, you're a slow reader.

• Between 200–300 WPM, you're an average reader.

• Between 300–600 WPM, you're a speed reader.

• Reading between 600–1000 WPM or above, you're a super speed reader.

By learning to read faster, you will become more focused and as such, have greater comprehension.

1.1.3 Read faster without training

Your inner voice slows you down

Having learned to read out loud at a very early age – and having gained a good proficiency – the teacher then tells you to read silently. The outcome of this exercise is that your voice gets trapped inside your own head. Inevitably, this inner speech ends up limiting your reading speed, albeit, you fail to realise this. You believe that everyone experiences the same thing; however, you also understand that some people have the ability to read faster, which you determine must be a blessing from God. In fact, God supplied us all with the ability to silence this voice and read quicker.

That is what we will be doing here; improving your reading power.

Silence your inner voice

First let's see how the brain works.

If I start speaking slowly – but very slowly – you get bored.

If... I... start... to... speak... even... slower... it... becomes... so... boring... that... you... will... disengage.

But now if I speak rather quickly... you get more interested and things make more sense. Don't you agree?

That is exactly what happens when you read slowly. Soon enough you will get bored. If you learn to go faster you start using your mind's eye to create the images described in the book. By imagining them you become motivated and you are more likely to remember what you read because you remember ideas that you create in your mind. You don't, and I repeat, you don't necessarily remember the words in the book, but the ideas that you create in your mind. We think in pictures all the time but we don't realise that.

Going faster you stay engaged, and become more focused.

Just as with video games, you start a new game slowly. However, as you become accustomed to the game, you become faster and more efficient. This progress becomes more fun and you know that your brain will continue to learn and improve even quicker. I am certain that you will enjoy the exercises for speed reading and will adapt very quickly because they work just like video games.

Pay attention to the voice in your head; do you stop to take a breath like you are reading out loud? That is not necessary! Are you giving more emphasis to certain parts of the narrative?

You can read faster and it is not difficult. I will show you how.

To start, you will be learning to speak less mentally with fewer words in your mind. Just start to make a conscious effort to say only the bigger words inside your mind and don't waste your time saying the linking words like "and", "or", "but" or "the". They will not disappear from the paper and you will understand the whole text. You will probably save yourself 20–30% of your time by avoiding the words that are not charged with meaning. Just repeat mentally the bigger words and you will start speed reading; your focus will improve and you will be reading faster and faster the more you do it.

This may sound strange at first; however, inside your head, attempt the following chapter saying only the keywords while paying attention to the context. I'm sure that you will be surprised with your performance. The more you practise, the greater progress you will make.

Start saying the bigger words inside your head and avoid saying the linking words. See how much you can learn this way. I bet you will get the meaning of it without any extra effort. I will put a black mask over the linking words throughout the next few paragraphs. Almost 33% of words are hidden and I believe you will get the ideas quite easily. You can start now! This is the first attempt of reading 33% faster.

Go ahead, read 33% faster by saving time looking only at the important words I've selected for you.

How you shift gears

If ▮ brain was ▮ car it ▮ certainly be ▮ Ferrari. Now can ▮ imagine having ▮ beautiful red Ferrari ▮ driving everywhere ▮ first gear?

Even travelling ▮ another country, you are ▮ ▮ motorway holding ▮ ▮ traffic because you ▮ stuck ▮ first gear. The reason ▮ ▮ is ▮ you didn't learn ▮ to shift gears. But once ▮ learn it ▮ easier ▮ drive, ▮ spend less petrol, ▮ don't overheat ▮ engine ▮ ▮ get ▮ your destination ▮ faster.

▮ speed read ▮ will learn how ▮ shift gears ▮ it ▮ become easier ▮ read ▮ you ▮ spend less energy ▮ ▮ better comprehension.

In turn you ▮ become ▮ flexible ▮ reading different material. Slower for ▮ fictional romance ▮ – faster ▮ reading ▮ manual ▮ ▮ technical book. ▮ ▮, you may be slower ▮ reading complicated material, ▮ having greater ability ▮ read quickly when ▮ become familiar with ▮ subject. You ▮ be able ▮ scan ▮ text merely ▮ ▮ overview ▮ perhaps skim through ▮ emails ▮ efficiently.

▮ mind processes information ▮ quickly. ▮ if you don't give ▮ mind something interesting ▮ pay attention █, it ██ drift away ███ think about something else.

Your mind works ███ associations and ██ actual words in ██ text ██ be ██ trigger for ███ mind █ think about something else.

Let's say ███ you ██ reading █ book ███ mentions ██ word "travelling". By reading slowly ███ mind might begin █ wander ████ from ██ text ██ start thinking about ███ last holiday █ perhaps ███ a place ███ you want to go █. This can ███ occur, which results in █ lack █ concentration.

Would you be ████ focused ████ driving █ car at 10 miles ███ hour, or █ hundred miles ███ hour? Naturally, you █████ ██ more focused driving at █ hundred miles ███ hour. You might ██ able █ appreciate ███ beautiful landscape, however, you █████ focused on ███ road ahead.

Well done!

Early speed reading experiments

It dates from before the Second World War. The Royal Air Force had to train pilots to distinguish friendly planes from enemy forces in a very short space of time.

While in a situation of combat, it was necessary to acknowledge if the plane approaching from the rear was an enemy or an ally. Naturally, such behaviour and instincts were vital for survival.

They had many ways to expand peripheral vision and one method was to have pilots look at a cinema screen and flash images of different planes at a distance. The idea was to train them to recognise and remember a still image fast and precisely.

They flashed small pictures of planes for one second and the pilots could recognise them.

In one of the pictures they could see an image like this:

This is a Spitfire, a British war plane.

The groups of pilots were shown a new set of pictures for just one fifth of a second and they were surprised that they could recognise them so well.

A third set of pictures were shown for one tenth of a second and they could identify the planes, too.

The most amazing thing was that, after training, the pilots could identify the planes in less than one thirtieth of a second. According to RAF files, some of the top pilots would recognise a plane in one hundredth of a second, which is quite remarkable.

The trainers were so impressed with the results that they decided to expand the experiment and had a great idea:

What about flashing text, word by word, very quickly?

Would the pilots be able to read it?

They started flashing the words 50% or even 100% faster than the average reading speed and the pilots understood everything. After further training, some of them were able to read even faster.

The pilots couldn't read faster on paper like they did on the screen

But there was a problem. The pilots would read very fast from the screen because their eyes were stationary and the words were coming towards them. However, when they were given a book to read, they had to move their eyes across the lines and they didn't know where to stop, and subsequently, most of them reverted to the traditional way and started reading slowly again on paper.

The secret was in harnessing the power of the right side of the brain instead of reading slowly with the left side of the brain.

Try it yourself and read faster! No effort required.

Watch the demonstration if you want to see how clever your brain is. You will speed read on the spot.

Now you will be able to see what the pilots saw. I will flash images of planes in rapid succession and one of the images won't be a plane but an animal. This will prove that you can assimilate information very quickly.

After that you will be able to speed read as if by magic.

For example, if your reading speed is 200 WPM (words per minute) you should watch the video that will flash words at 210 WPM and 315 WPM. You will experience reading 50% faster, and I believe you will find 315 WPM easier than 210 WPM.

I believe that you will understand the whole thing at this fast pace. It's really incredible…

If you've taken the test already, you know how fast you are reading and will be surprised with the results. Sometimes numbers talk louder than words.

If you didn't take the test, go to the webpage below to test yourself; if you've done it already, just skip the following line.

www.thespeedreadingcoach.com/test

Watch the planes and read faster on the spot.

Go to this webpage and select the appropriate video to watch based on your reading speed. Push play, and relax… Try a faster speed to test yourself.

www.thespeedreadingcoach.com/flash

Well done, you are a speed reader already! Just do the maths to see how much faster you can read. Keep track of your improvement on your Control Sheet on page 58 under "Fastest Zap" or write it down on your diary.

Congratulations!!!

Did you watch the summarised version of The 7 Habits of Highly Effective People by Stephen Covey?

I have prepared it to be flashed 500 WPM. If you watch, it will only take you less than seven minutes to understand and learn the essential ideas from the book. This is really a no-brainer if you want to become highly effective.

It is like a video game; the more you play, the easier it gets. It will also help you to expand your peripheral vision, which will help you read any text faster.

I'm creating a library of summaries of great books so you can read them super-fast.

After watching the videos, you can also start using the software to read faster from your screen. It is FREE and very effective in helping your mind start accepting information at a faster pace. It will help you read normal text too.

I recommend you give it a try.

Just copy and paste the material you want to read inside a box, select the speed you want to read it at and then it flashes the words in a very effective way. You don't even realise that you're reading at a faster speed!

Check my website for the Free software that will help you perform better than ever.

Go to the following page:

ALEX GARCEZ

www.thespeedreadingcoach.com/freesoftware

Now I will start to explain to you how to speed read a
normal text without the software.

I'm sure that you are going to love it!

PART 2 - USE A POINTER TO READ FASTER EASILY

"Contrary to popular belief, there is no such thing as an educated person. You are either learning or you are not."

Bob Proctor

By reading this chapter, you can expect to improve your reading speed from 10-30% or more... try this out!

Time to read this chapter

at 100 wpm	23 min
at 200 wpm	12 min
at 300 wpm	8 min
at 400 wpm	6 min
at 500 wpm	5 min
at 600 wpm	4 min
at 700 wpm	3 min
at 800 wpm	3 min
at 900 wpm	3 min
at 1000 wpm	2 min

1.2.1 Preview and review

To preview a book it is important to understand that you should have a pretty good idea why you are going to read that book. This should set your purpose to read it. I flick through it, read the back cover, table of contents and a little from a couple of chapters. Finally, I look at the book and I have a feeling if I should read that book or not. And then I follow my instincts.

Reading a great book means that you read that book and the timing was right.

By reading a book with a purpose or intention behind it, you will find many good things in any book because you are looking for them. I aim to find just one good idea from reading one whole book. If I have one great idea while reading, I might consider it a great book.

If you find the answer to the question you had when you got ready to read, you could also stop reading the book altogether and start a new one. You will see a lot of connections in your life by opening more books.

Then comes the review, which means taking notes, creating Mind Maps and creating a summary.

You remember more of what you read if you write the summary using your own words, which is active and much better than copying the words of the author.

It is important to have a voice, and this voice should be exercised not only by praising but also by criticising and having an opinion about the world. Some people will like your ideas, follow your thoughts and you will in turn, have a following.

1.2.2 Secrets to guide your eyes using your pointer, pen or fingertip

Keep reading and saying only the bigger words inside your mind; did you forget to do it?

Avoid verbalising the small and linking words. This way you will develop your reading speed and get used to this new way to improve your reading performance. Practise this little trick and you will be surprised to find that you increase your reading speed by 20% or more.

Knowing that you can absorb information faster, I would like to invite you to try something very simple, yet very powerful.

The idea is to use a pointer to help you move faster while reading. By using a pointer, you will start to get more focused.

Your eyes naturally follow motion, so moving your pointer under the line you are reading will help you to go faster because you will stop lingering for too long on each line and will also avoid regression.

You will make your eyes glide smoothly along the lines of text.

By giving your eyes something to focus on, you can create a rhythm to your reading and increase your reading speed.

Just understanding this alone will help you improve your reading speed by 10–30%.

Children begin pointing out words as they learn to read. However, as they develop their skills, they are discouraged from pointing out each word as that slows down their ability to read with greater efficiency.

To get started you should use a pointer every time you read anything because it will help you increase your reading speed from now on.

Pick up a book that you are interested in and want to use for your practice. It is best if it is non-fiction because you know a lot of the content already and will be surprised how much repetition you can see in a factual book. It is best if the book is not too technical, without too many bullet points, graphs and charts, as it really needs to be continual text. Biographies can be factual but they are not a great choice to start with. Preferably, a book that contains an average of 10 words on each line will enable you to read with greater precision. If it is more or less, then that is fine, however, if you are using a digital format, then make the pages big enough to have an average of 10 words per line.

It is OK to use a book you have already read. This is to learn the techniques and be confident applying them. Once you have practised reading this way, you will naturally apply what you've learnt to any material you read and become more flexible to reading faster.

If English is not your first language, you may also like to use books in your mother tongue; some people find it easier to learn this way and then apply it to written English.

The best option would be to keep reading this book and applying the techniques you learn while you read. I recommend that you read each chapter twice, if you feel the need to, so you don't get afraid of missing anything because you know you will be reading that chapter again. Give it a go and check the results later. I'm sure you will be surprised at how quickly you progress.

If you prefer to choose another book to practise, then please choose an easy book to read.

Now you need to choose a pointer. A long pointer like a bamboo skewer, a drinking straw or a chopstick is best. You can always use your fingers to make the pointer slide line by line instead of moving your whole arm to move the pointer around. A long pointer is comfortable but you can also use a pen or even your fingertip. Moving your finger around, you will notice that your arm will feel tired quite quickly, but it will work the same.

Start reading with a pointer, and just let yourself flow. Take in the information and move on.

If you need to say any words in your head, it makes sense to say the big and important ones. Try not to linger too much there. Whenever you see linking words avoid saying them. Linking words are just like wallpaper, they don't hold the house together they only make it look good. They will link the ideas of the keywords but you don't need to say them in your head to be able to understand the whole message of a paragraph or a chapter.

Now, take a pointer or a pen and keep reading this book with it. Just push yourself a little bit to help you go faster and stop lingering for too long on the words.

You can start now!

Are you already using a pointer? That's great!

Give it a try; this is the beginning of your training. It is easy and it will help you perform better from now on.

I believe that you will feel like creating a pace for yourself and the information will start flowing in, at a different speed. It will feel like you understand more with less effort.

This is the magic of using a pointer.

1.2.3 Skipping back to re-read is a waste of time

You will avoid skipping back if you understand this simple idea. Based on experience, I estimate that we skip back to re-read for about 30% of the time. If you become more focused and start skipping back only 10% of the time, you will be reading 20% faster without even starting to apply the techniques.

The first thing to start changing, is your habit of skipping back and re-reading something you didn't understand.

From this point on, I would advise you to stop going back whenever you don't understand something you read. If you don't understand, keep moving forward as much as you can and I would suggest you read until the end of the page before going back. The information you've missed is very likely to come back again before the end of the page you are reading or it will appear in discussion form throughout the book using words or expressions that are more familiar to you. So don't panic and keep moving forward.

If you know that you can always go back, you don't get focused and become distracted. The habit of going back undermines your confidence and you end up getting bored and stop reading the book or text because you don't become engaged enough.

Of course, you are free to skip back but try not to and keep your mind switched on to engage again and follow the train of thought.

So, skip back only if it is very important to do so.

Don't skip back every one or two lines. Tension creates engagement and fluidity to understand the main idea of a text. By the end of the page, your mind will get back on track and you will get most of the content anyway.

If we make a comparison between reading a book and watching a film, I would point out some important correlations:

I'm from Brazil and I've been living in London for more than 16 years. Whenever I'm watching a film, I really need to pay attention because there are so many accents that come with new regional words and expressions that make it impossible to understand everything I listen to on TV. It is also very difficult to grasp certain lyrics in music and quite often I miss bits of information in face-to-face communication when the person uses words that I'm unfamiliar with.

The *Oxford English Dictionary* lists more than 750,000 words; and according to the Google/Harvard Study, there are more than 1,020,000 words in the English language, and each word can have multiple meanings. I found on the Internet that hundreds of thousands of technical and scientific terms remain uncatalogued, which is easy to imagine and hard to verify. The English *Wikipedia* has 5.1 million articles (2016) and it averages 800 new articles per day. So, now I know that even if I wanted to understand everything that I see on television or a film, it would be impossible for me or any other native speaker, too. There will always be some accents that we find difficult to understand. We are soaking in cultures that change words and create expressions. If I am watching a movie and I don't understand what someone is saying, I carry on watching it without pausing and I catch up on the plot later. Sometimes I try to understand that weird accent from Scotland and I understand what I can. I know, my accent is weird, too. I'm Brazilian. So there will always be noise in the communication because more and more people are learning how to speak English.

Depending on your profession and social class, you will develop a particular vocabulary that will help you expand yourself in new areas of knowledge. A clever doctor might read a simple brochure for financial services and it will appear to him to be a completely different world, which is why we hire advisors so they can translate the language to us and we can make a wise decision. It's all down to vocabulary.

Sometimes I am watching a film on TV and I go to the kitchen during the commercial break to get something to snack on and I get back more than three minutes later. Do I get desperate for missing part of the film? Not that much. Do I switch the television off because I've missed three minutes? No, I carry on and try to catch up with the film and I imagine you do the same.

Whenever you start reading a non-fiction book, you should apply the same principle of keeping going. If you miss something that doesn't seem to be very important, you could just carry on and try to catch up with the development of the book and be aware that if you miss three minutes of a film, it would equal to around three pages that you've skipped. The author will be very likely to repeat the same idea in different words because they want to explain something very well to a big audience and this takes repetition. Normally, books do not have a *Sherlock Holmes* plot that if you miss one tiny detail you will be missing an important clue to the mystery. The authors are on your side and will help you understand a concept using examples and analogies so keep your cool and read forward as much as you can.

So, just remember that we can't understand it all because there are more than one million words in the English language and, according to the Global

Language Monitor, a new word is created every 98 minutes. We use around 3,000 words for ordinary conversation. For more advanced conversation you will use 5,000 but you will need more than just the words! You need context and expressions, too.

According to David Crystal, a world-renowned expert on the English language, a person starting school knows 500-6,000 words; before starting a degree they would know 50,000 words, and by taking a degree they would know 50-75,000. Most of these words are passive vocabulary, which means that they might understand the words but will never use them.

According to Professor Alexander Arguelles, a language learning expert fluent in eleven languages, the number of words we know grows with education and I quote his findings below:

"250 words constitute the essential core of a language, those without which you cannot construct any sentence.

750 words constitute those that are used every single day by every person who speaks the language.

2,500 words constitute those that should enable you to express everything you could possibly want to say, albeit, often by awkward circumlocutions.

5,000 words constitute the active vocabulary of native speakers without higher education.

10,000 words constitute the active vocabulary of native speakers with higher education.

20,000 words constitute what you need to recognize passively in order to read, understand, and enjoy a work of literature such as a novel by a notable author.

The maddening thing about these numbers and statistics is that they are impossible to pin down precisely and thus they vary from source to source."

The following graph is a simplistic representation of vocabulary and the number of words in the English language.

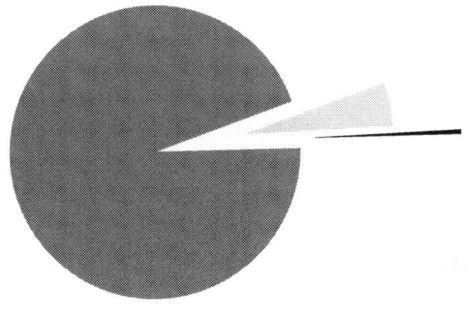

0.5% – Native basic vocabulary - 5,000 words
5% – Native vocabulary after Degree - 50,000 words
94.25% – Native with Degree will not learn
1,000,000 words

Learn vocabulary

Relax and read with a purpose. If you read a whole book and find just one great idea that you can implement in your life or work, then the book was really useful. So read and keep searching for that one good idea. It might happen that you will find more than one, but the intention is to read actively instead of reading passively. If you have a question in your mind you will be able to make your own conclusions and will get the big picture anyway. New words will come and go; just pay attention to the message and look up a word that starts appearing quite often. There is a way to learn and remember new words that I will explain when I talk about the right side of the brain in my next book.

Keep reading with your pointer because it will help you to start going faster and you will get more focused while reading.

EXPERIENCE FOUR RHYTHMS TO READ

"Change the way you look at things and the things you look at will change…"

Wayne Dyer

By reading this chapter you can expect to improve your reading speed from 20–90% or more!

Time to read this chapter

at 100 wpm	53 min
at 200 wpm	27 min
at 300 wpm	18 min
at 400 wpm	13 min
at 500 wpm	11 min
at 600 wpm	9 min
at 700 wpm	8 min
at 800 wpm	7 min
at 900 wpm	6 min
at 1000 wpm	5 min

2.1 Easy practice with pointer and rhythm

Just by using a pointer, I believe that even at this stage you will be faster already. It might be hard to register 5% or 10% improvement, but if you are 20% or 30% faster, you have probably noticed that you are not skipping back so much to re-read and are moving along the lines more smoothly.

Keep using the pointer while reading the next set of instructions. Your eyes will get used to the new system in no time at all. It's important to synchronise your eyes and your hand. The results will speak for themselves.

Keep reading with your pointer.

If you are right-handed, start moving your pointer with your left hand. This way you will be using the right side of the brain and the results will be even better. I will explain about the right side of the brain in more detail later. If you are left-handed, keep using your left hand.

If you didn't like switching hands at all you can keep using your right hand.

Your brain is amazing, and if I would compare it with a real machine, I would say it is a Red Ferrari.

Most people have a Ferrari for a brain but they go everywhere in first gear. This is a waste of time and petrol and you will strain the engine...

Now you will start to shift gears and will start to go faster with less effort and more comprehension will follow.

Remember that you always start in first gear and then you shift gears up as you go along. Go faster when you can but if you find difficult terrain, you slow down to third, second or first gear again. Be flexible and remember that your gear stick is the pointer that you have in your hands.

Now we will start shifting gears...

You will be using a metronome, which is a little machine, software or App used by musicians to help them play music at exactly the right pace by following a rhythm. If you play the piano, drums, guitar or any other instrument, you are probably familiar with it. If you have never heard of it before, it is easy to understand. You can learn how to play a song, but if you play it too fast or too slow, it won't sound good. So, the metronome will help you play at a constant rhythm and once you get used to the clicking sound, your fingers will start moving with the rhythm automatically. At this point you can switch the metronome off and you will be playing the song at the right pace.

2.2 On your mark

Before I show you how to use the metronome to instantly improve your reading speed, I want to share an interesting way to boost your mental power.

We all feel a little insecure before trying something for the first time, so I want to share a scientific way that can help you become more assertive.

Boost your confidence to succeed in two minutes flat

Amy Cuddy is a social psychologist, and she noticed that men and women that occupy a position of power usually have higher testosterone levels. Higher testosterone levels are associated with confidence and risk taking. They also have lower levels of cortisol, which reflects a lower level of stress.

She observed that powerful people have body language that displays their dominance. They find ways to take more space by expanding the space their bodies take up. Examples of these power poses are:

• Sit down on a chair, put your feet on the table and put your hands behind your head.

• Someone celebrating their victory in an athletic competition would open their arms while reaching for the skies and tilting their heads up.

• Stand tall, shoulders back, chest out, spread your legs and put your hands on your hips like the Wonder Woman or Superman.

Just by sitting down on your chair and spreading your arms out, or over the back of your chair, will show your dominance.

This discovery is the result of a series of studies. In one study a group of men and women were interviewed for a job. Half of the participants held a power pose for two minutes, just before the interview, and a saliva sample was taken before and after.

The other half were instructed to sit down with their legs together and make themselves smaller. Some would slouch with their shoulders rolled inwards, which is the typical posture of someone using their mobile phone. The second group stayed in this position for two minutes, and a saliva sample was taken before and after.

The surprising result of this study is that the people that held a power pose before the interview were more relaxed, assertive and confident. The interviewers wanted to hire the ones that were power posing and also evaluated them more positively than those candidates that were making themselves smaller before the interview. The results also showed that those that were power posing immediately raised their testosterone level by 20% and lowered their stress by dropping their cortisol level by 25%. The group that was scrunched up had opposite results by lowering their testosterone by 10% and showed a raise in their anxiety by a 15% increase in their cortisol.

So, now that you are about to try something new, you will perform much better if you have a higher level of confidence and a lower level of anxiety. I am now inviting you to choose a power pose and hold it for two minutes before you start the speed reading exercise. It will rapidly change your hormone levels and also make you perform better at reading.

You will boost your confidence, enthusiasm and your willingness to take risks instantly. You will feel like you are doing the right thing, will adapt to the new reading speeds with ease and will have a better comprehension of the text.

So, pause for a couple of minutes before doing the exercise with the metronome and the pointer. This is a decisive moment! You will build your confidence to read faster and the results can last a lifetime. Choose a power pose and feel the power growing inside yourself. If you decide to go to the kitchen to make a coffee, before you hold the power pose, walk like a champion would walk. You will definitely feel the difference.

Remember that this is a strategy that you can use anytime you want to be more assertive and confident.

If you want to watch Amy Cuddy explaining the *Power Posing* experiment in a TED Talk, go to the website below and search for her name. She also wrote a fantastic book called *Presence.*

www.ted.com

Now you are ready to speed read!

2.3 Get set

How to read faster using the metronome

You will have to go to the webpage below for this exercise.

www.thespeedreadingcoach.com/audio

Once you are there, you will play the video that is suitable for you, based on the results of your reading speed tests.

For example, if your average reading speed was 210 words per minute, you will play the video with 20, 25 and 30 beats per minute (BPM). This video plays all three rhythms in sequence. The first rhythm is intended to be close to your actual reading speed.

Please choose the appropriate video to suit you.

You need to follow the rhythm and read one line per beat. Considering that every line has 10 words on average, you will be reading at a speed of 200 WPM. Just multiply the rhythm by the average number of words per line in your book to know at which speed you are reading.

You can practise the exercise by continuing to read this book or choose a book that has on average 10 words per line to make things easier.

The rhythms will start at 20 beats per minute, which means that you will hear 20 little "clicks" in one minute, like a clock ticking very slowly.

You should be using your pointer to help you keep up with the pace and will read one full line at every single beat. Move the pointer, under the words, from the beginning to the end of the line slowly and in sync with the rhythm. Every time you hear the "click" you should start a new line, so you will cover one line for each "click". If you don't like using the pointer you can try with your fingertip instead.

You will start reading at 200 WPM. You need to keep up with the rhythm for two minutes to get the hang of it. I will increase the speed from 20 to 25 and to 30 BPM. Your left side of the brain will find it difficult to follow, so your right side of the brain will kick in and start giving you the comprehension that you want. This will happen more so because you will start to expand you peripheral vision and will be able to see and understand more words at every fixation.

After reading at 200 WPM for two minutes, I will then increase the pace to 25 beats per minute or 250 WPM, after which time, you shall try to read for two minutes at 300 WPM, which is 50% faster than 200 WPM.

If you have a shorter line at the end of a paragraph, spread all the time you have in that line and linger there so that you keep in sync with the rhythm.

It is best if you move your fingers and hand instead of moving your whole arm to move your pointer. Less energy spent moving your body will result in greater comprehension.

Once you start playing the metronome, you will be able to read one line per beat.

At the beginning of every new rhythm you will have to get used to it, and in a little while your comprehension will start to improve.

If you don't have good comprehension don't worry, just keep up with the exercise to get comfortable at one reading speed. You will understand the mechanics of reading faster in the next few chapters and your performance will keep improving as you learn more about your reading skill.

2.4 The secret sauce

Now I am going to share with you one of the greatest secrets of this book. As you start to read faster, your comprehension will decrease. Comprehension will only arise as a result of you being stable in one of the rhythms. You might be surprised to notice that a faster pace might give you better understanding than a slower one, so try them all. Some people need just a few minutes to adjust to a new pace, while others might take a few hours.

Choose to focus and understand. I tell you that you can!!!

Get ready with your pointer and please remember:

- To take a deep breath and relax while reading.

- Don't be anxious to learn everything at once.

- If you don't understand everything, it is OK, just keep up with the rhythm and comprehension will follow as a result.

2.5 Go!

Keep using your pointer and play the video that suits you on the webpage below to start reading with the metronome. Start it now!

www.thespeedreadingcoach.com/audio

I recommend you choose another book of your choice for the practice, but you can carry on reading this book.

These six minutes have changed many people's lives. You will have the first experience of reading at three different speeds. Everything is very new and you are just stretching your power to digest information at a different pace. You will start changing gears in your mind.

This is just the beginning!

After having your first experience with the metronome, I want you to think about it. Which pace worked best for you?

Each person will achieve different results. Those who begin the course starting at 200 WPM might feel confident to increase their reading capability while improving on their overall comprehension to 300 WPM. It can take some time to gain full understanding; however, as long as you stay in one particular rhythm long enough, your brain will find a way to give you the perception you deserve.

It is fascinating to me when someone goes from 200 WPM, to 500 or even 600 WPM, with great comprehension. To do this requires having the ability to relax and as the peripheral vision expands, the results can be outstanding. This is the moment when the left side of the brain gives up full control and starts to support the reading process, while the right side takes over. The act of reading becomes a whole-brain activity.

This is the first time you have experienced this accelerated way of reading, and you will develop more and more with continuous practice.

Once you finish listening to your video, you can then decide which speed you liked the most.

Go to the webpage below to listen to a free metronome online, and select the new rhythm to read your book.

http://a.bestmetronome.com

The best metronome you can get is a free App called **Pro Metronome**, which is available for iOS and Android.

Download the App and select the rhythm that will help you get consistent in one single reading speed.

The App is great because you can speed up the beats one notch at a time and get the perfect rhythm to read any text.

This is how the **Pro Metronome** App looks like:

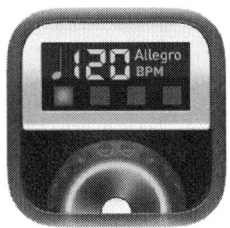

If you want to programme a sequence of beats to suit your needs you can upgrade to the *Practice Mode* £0.79 (this is one of seven possible upgrades). Open it by clicking a little clock at the bottom of the screen. You will be able to create a sequence of rhythms like the examples below by choosing the *Automator* and *By Time,* once you are inside the *Practice Mode*.

- 15, 20, 25, 30 beats per minute, that will play in sequence. Six minutes each.

- 45, 55, 65, 75 beats per minute, that will play in sequence. Five minutes each.

I have many sequences to choose from on my website, but by upgrading the App you can change the sequences as much as you like. This way you will have more control on finding the best possible rhythm to improve your speed and achieve good comprehension.

Don't forget to use your pointer and you will keep improving as you read this book.

2.6 Raising your comprehension

Your brain is prepared to understand whole expressions at once, so stop holding on to individual words and start to recognise expressions. Soon enough you will start to foresee the future and will reach the conclusion before the author reveals their own point of view.

Using the metronome, you will notice that you can follow the new pace; however, your comprehension suffers a lot, and therefore, you can't link everything together in your mind because it will seem too quick at first.

The brain is so clever that if you can't perform a task well, it will find a way to get the best results. And the results come fast.

The metronome goes from 30–100+ beats per minute, so don't be nervous as it is possible to read at 1000 WPM and beyond. This can be achieved when you are reading something that you feel comfortable with, which is the result of practising with the metronome. The more you practise, the better the comprehension. Imagine being inside a dark room. For a moment, you can't see a thing. However, after two or three minutes, you begin to get used to the dark and start to see. Reading faster works in much the same way. The more you practise, the more consistent you become, and the greater your comprehension will be.

The following graph illustrates that whenever you go faster your comprehension drops. But keep your speed stable and your comprehension will get better and better until you can understand everything that is relevant to you.

Comprehension level drops when you start to read faster and increases if you keep reading at a certain speed for some time.

Comprehension in %

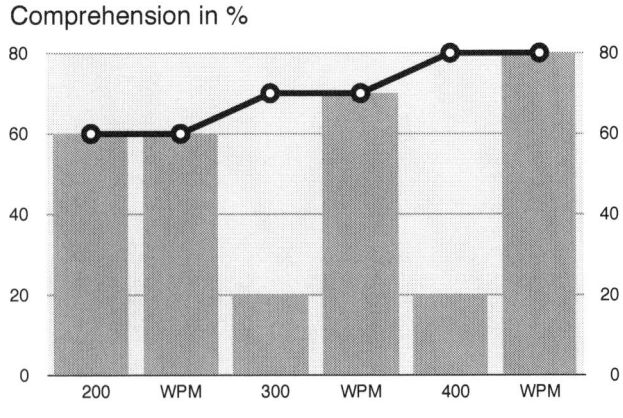

Reading speed in Words Per Minute

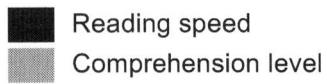
Reading speed
Comprehension level

We filter information all the time so you will remember things that are relevant to you. You will never remember everything written in a book, as that is not possible.

A lot of text is just padding and doesn't come with much content; it is just light commentary about what the author is about to present you with, so learn how to skim through parts that you might think are not relevant. Don't feel guilty about jumping around if you are reading a non-fiction book. You should have a purpose and look for things that are important to you.

You can choose the rhythm that you are most comfortable with whilst you are reading. Read for around half an hour or so. You can always change the track if you wish.

Knowing that your comprehension levels will drop if you go faster will help you to relax with the knowledge that such levels will increase if you spend enough time reading at that very same speed. Don't be anxious; read for some time with your metronome.

Continue to practise with the metronome.

2.7 Many subjects will not interest you, but

If you are talking to a group of friends, you will feel connected with the information that is meaningful to you. Sometimes, however, you will disconnect because someone is talking about a subject that you are not interested in at all and your mind switches off. Let's say that someone is talking about their kids and you are not really interested in them because you don't have any children and can't relate to their drama. You disconnect and don't pay attention to what they are saying because your mind is filtering reality according to your own way of seeing the world. If you *are* interested in children there will be many subjects that won't attract you like politics, football, fashion or the Middle East conflict. You keep learning certain subjects and others you simply ignore.

We filter information all the time with the RAS

There is a part of our brain called the Reticular Activating System (RAS) that gives us the ability to consciously focus our attention on something. In addition, the RAS acts as a filter; dampening down the effect of repeated stimuli such as loud noises or visual pollution, helping to prevent the senses from being overloaded. In fact, the RAS helps us to function in life by constantly deleting, distorting and generalising information to be able to cope with two million bits of information that reach our five senses and our conscious and unconscious mind every second.

Can you remember a time when you were planning to buy a new car? Maybe a Mercedes Benz for example; suddenly you see so many Mercedes around that it can be quite overwhelming. The same might be said for women who are pregnant – they notice lots of other women who are pregnant everywhere they go.

Have you had the experience of learning a new word and suddenly you open a book and there it is again. Moreover, you might switch on the radio and you hear that same word repeated yet again. That is the RAS that stopped filtering that strange word by giving it meaning and now it appears in your virtual landscape.

So, by filtering information you are constantly selecting to pay attention to certain things and deleting other items from your conscious awareness. In the same way, you will not understand many things in a book or text because your RAS automatically erases information that you don't relate to.

Based on that observation, I want to reinforce that you should avoid skipping back to re-read as much as you can because your RAS will also find relevant information for you. I believe that it makes more sense now.

You can get frustrated because you don't have enough vocabulary. But remember, if you are learning a subject you should expect to find new words in the same way you know that the author will explain the new concepts in different ways, and then you will be able to grasp the information. It is therefore useful to know, that to learn any subject, you will have to learn new words and will need to improve your vocabulary. The English language has more words than any other language. Just to put it into perspective we have at least four times more words than Shakespeare had available in the 17th Century (according to Karl Fisch and Scott McLeod. YouTube: Did you know? Shift happens). Remember that it is not only the number of words that make a language but the number of new expressions too.

A solicitor has a different vocabulary from a doctor or a stock-broker. They just happen to know more words as a perk of their trade. Some words they've learnt without much explanation and others they had to ask someone or they have looked up in a dictionary.

We are all limited by our ignorance and you will expand your experience in this world if you add new words to your vocabulary.

100% Comprehension doesn't exist

Pareto was a mathematician who created the well-known *Pareto Principle*, which is also known as the 80–20 rule. It states that in general, 80% of the effects come from 20% of the causes. This principle can be applied to many fields and just to give you an example, I could say that 80% of your profits come from 20% of your customers. This is true for a big proportion of businesses. Now applying the same principle to books I could say that 80% of the important information will come from 20% of the content of a book.

Generally speaking, non-fiction books are not a detective story. You may think that if you miss a little detail you will jeopardise the whole book but you won't.

Relax, I believe that 20–50% of what you read is just padding! Hold on, it's not what you think!

I wrote this book with a few key messages and I repeat myself 20-50% to reinforce the main ideas with theory, history, examples, stories and practice.

I like the analogy of thinking that each chapter of a book is a beautiful room in a house. The author will guide you through many long corridors to show you each room. The corridor might have paintings on the wall, carpets, flowers and light features and you glance at them but don't pay full attention to these details because you are really interested in the room you are about to enter. Whenever you enter the room you might be enchanted by it and all the details that make it so special. The room will make a big impression on you. So focus on the room and don't worry too much if you don't remember the details of the corridor.

Even if you score 100% on a comprehension test you cannot say that you know 100% of that subject because our mind filters reality. So, as a result we see a reality that is moulded with our preconceptions and is focused on our interests.

It is incredible that we can only see what we are programmed to see. All those advertisements for broadband didn't really exist until I decided to look for a new provider. They are not there because I can't see them. Do you understand how it works?

My advice is that you shouldn't be so hard on yourself while reading because 100% comprehension doesn't exist. You will always stumble on a new word or expression, but you shouldn't be any less motivated to go ahead.

If you find a golden concept in a chapter of a book, it will be a concept that you will find the meaning of even if you miss a little bit here and there. I'm not advocating being superficial. I'm just aware of our limitations and extreme standards that we think we can achieve. I just want you to relax. Keep reading in search for new ideas or concepts. I hope you can enjoy reading more because an average book will become a great book if the timing for reading it is right. So read more and progress in life faster.

2.8 See your blind spot here. It exists...

Sometimes we have a psychological blind spot and we can't see our glasses while they are just in front of us. What you might not know is that there is a real blind spot on each of our eyes. In the back of our eyes there is a specific place where there are no light detection sensors because that area is occupied by the nerves that link the eyes to the brain.

To see what I mean, observe the following picture. Just cover your left eye with your hand and stare at the letter X at all times. Your right eye should be straight in front of the letter X. Slowly move closer to the X, until the moment that the rabbit disappears completely from your field of vision – as if by magic. This is because your eyes can't see from that angle and the blind spot hides the rabbit.

X

If you can't find your keys in the morning, you have a mental blind spot. Then a relative comes and picks up the keys from under your nose and you are astonished, realising that the keys were in front of you all that time and you couldn't see them. This is called "scotoma".

In the same way, you have a mental blind spot if you can't see certain matters in life because you don't pay them attention. Your blind spot can be football, the stock market, gossip magazines or any other area you know very little about and there are areas of knowledge you are not even aware that exist.

There is a lot to learn in this world. You can create a window of interest in your life by deciding on the areas that you wish to learn more about. Books are a perfect source of education, and currently I'm working on creating the books of the future. They are dynamic and come in many sizes to suit your lifestyle and preferences of media. You will soon be able to read and watch the best non-fiction books ever, in a format that will fascinate you.

Each one of us see the world in a different way

The Reticular Activating System is responsible for opening these windows of perception so you can see the world in a very particular way. The RAS gives you focus and if you have a question in your mind, it will start looking for an answer inside your memory banks and will be searching for the answer at all times and places. This is important because if your purpose is to read and focus your attention on *"What is in it for you"*, you will find something that you can apply and take advantage of.

But if you don't start reading actively, you will end up reading the whole text and remember very little of it. So, the tip is to "Think" of a reason or outcome when you get a book to read. The purpose doesn't have to be directly connected to the subject you are reading. You will find what you are after.

For example, if you are frustrated with your meetings at work, you can focus your attention on finding better ways to run them. You might find the answer reading a magazine at the dentist or reading a book about entrepreneurship.

This is the RAS in action. Having a purpose, directs your judgment in a way that will give you more and more arguments to protect or develop your point of view. If you support a football team or a political party, you already know that you see reality very differently from your opponents. We think things are good while they think things are bad, and vice-versa.

As a general rule, you will learn much more from a conversation or a book if you know what kind of information you are after, because you start using your inquisitive mind instead of reading passively.

I've heard some successful people say that:

"The quality of your life will be directly connected to the quality of your questions."

I believe that you will be more successful if you ask better questions. I think this is a great way of thinking.

Because we watch too much television, we end up getting used to receiving information in a very passive way.

Studies have shown that watching TV stimulates the production of low alpha waves in the brain, which are usually associated with meditative states. While meditation can promote insights and relaxation, watching a lot of television promotes unfocused daydreaming and it can weaken your power to focus (no wonder people are more suggestible while watching TV).

I haven't had a TV for many years now, however, there was a time when I was hooked on it. If you keep watching television for too long every day, you are probably addicted to it. If you are a parent, please consider controlling the amount of TV your children watch.

On the other hand, reading stimulates your creativity, imagination and memory.

2.9 Developing your focus

Persistence is fundamental to focusing your mind.

When I read *Outliers* by Malcolm Gladwell, I learned that most people who succeed are those from families or cultures that teach people to persist at what they are doing for longer. For example, solving a maths problem before giving up on the task.

It makes a big difference if you only spend 20 seconds before giving up than if you spend two minutes before asking for help. Those that go a little bit further – go all the way and persist – will achieve great results. If you look for the answer you will find it.

If you persist and read a book with a purpose, you will use the book to help you find a solution for any problem or challenge you might have. Have an objective to read and you will be reading actively instead of reading passively and getting distracted.

Meditation can help you read faster

Another way to harness your mind power, develop your focus and improve your reading performance is to practice meditation.

After many years dabbling with meditation, I decided to study it properly by jumping into the deep end and enrolling myself on a ten-day silent meditation retreat. To sit down on the floor for ten hours a day, for ten consecutive days was a gruelling experience, but to my surprise, I learnt how to really focus my mind. As a result, I had the privilege of understanding the world from a new level of consciousness and experienced a state of ecstasy I didn't know existed.

Fortunately, I found new ways to achieve deep levels of meditation that are easily accessible to someone without any previous training, and I recommend some of the best ones on the webpage below.

www.thespeedreadingcoach.com/meditation

PART 1 - ACHIEVE GOOD COMPREHENSION

"It is not the strongest that survives, nor the most intelligent. It's the one that is most adaptable to change."

Charles Darwin

By reading this chapter you can expect to improve your reading speed by a further 10–50%, so why not try.

Time to read this chapter

at 100 wpm	23 min
at 200 wpm	11 min
at 300 wpm	8 min
at 400 wpm	6 min
at 500 wpm	5 min
at 600 wpm	4 min
at 700 wpm	3 min
at 800 wpm	3 min
at 900 wpm	3 min
at 1000 wpm	2 min

3.1.1 Watch the eye tracker in action

Your eyes move in strange patterns to read, so in a moment I will show you the eye tracker in action and you will see a person's strategy to read in real time. It is an incredible sight! But before I do, I will show you the mechanics of reading so you will understand how it is possible to read faster.

First you need to know how your eyes work.

Your eyes can see things clearly when you hold them still. If an object is still, the eyes must be also still to be able to see it, and if the object is moving, the eyes must move with the object to be able to see it clearly.

If you pay attention to a person reading the paper or looking at a computer screen, you will notice that their eyes keep jumping throughout the lines.

Your eyes keep shifting and focusing on to every single thing they want to see clearly. In fact, they change focus or move around once per second.

The text on the next page shows the eye movement while reading.

The dots are the places where your eyes stop while reading. Notice that they actually stop five or six times on each line of text.

If you prefer to watch a video with real time eye movement, then please go to the link below and see how your eyes behave while you read. I think it is incredible.

The eye tracker combines software and cameras that focus on the eyes of a person so it can show precisely where the person is looking at. The demonstration is very important to watch because you will see how you read in real time and how you can get distracted because of involuntary eye movements. Go to the webpage below to watch it.

www.thespeedreadingcoach.com/eyetracker

Your eyes stop far too many times per line to be efficient

I bet you are surprised to have seen the eyes moving while reading. When you read, it is important to synchronise the speed by following each word with the movement of your eyes. Your eyes keep moving their central focus and stop every second.

Because you are reading at the same speed that you talk, you have no reason to move your eyes faster.

Typically, they would stop six times on each line; like in the following paragraph, if you were reading at around 250 WPM:

.   .   .   .   .   .

Read faster to get more focused and enjoy your book.

You will see all the words in sequence and will stop six times over the line. You don't read each line in a smooth fashion; in fact, your eyes will be jerking from one group of words to the next.

Stop less and you will see more

Now, to speed read I will help you go faster, your eyes will be stopping fewer times on each line and you can still see and understand all the words.

If you were to stop six times on each line, the next step that I will show you is how to stop just three times, and as a result, you will be reading 100% faster. Simple isn't it? If you end up stopping only twice on each line you will be reading 200% faster. You will get used to expanding your peripheral vision and instead of seeing two or three words every time you stop, you will start seeing three, four or even five words at a time. Because they are in perfect sequence, you will understand the meaning without much effort. It is just a matter of practising a little bit and your brain will get used to it.

It is also interesting to notice that you will overlap your field of vision every time that you move from one fixation point to the next, so you see the words you are reading at least two times while reading a typical line. What a waste of time.

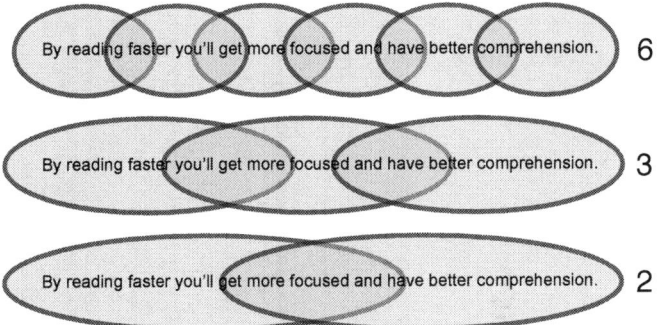

Now stop for less time each time you glance

The second way to enhance your reading speed is by jumping ahead as soon as you get a glimpse of the words. Just move faster and your brain will catch up and start enabling your comprehension. Just like it is difficult to play a video game in the first few minutes, it then gets much easier and you keep chasing the performance and speed. You can get tired eventually but it is stimulating to go faster.

When you read a line, the eyes keep jumping and stopping. The jumps take almost no time, but the fixations can take anything from one and a half seconds to one quarter of a second.

This way the eye takes short gulps of information; in between it is not actually seeing anything, it is moving from one point to another. We don't notice these jumps because the information is held over in the brain and integrated from one fixation to the next, so that we can perceive a smooth flow. The eye is rarely still for more than a couple of seconds. Even if you feel the eye is completely still by looking at a question mark, it will in fact be making some small movements around the point. If the eyes were not constantly moving in this way and making new fixations, the image would rapidly get fuzzy.

A slow reader, who pauses at every word and skips back reading the same word two or three times, will not be able to understand much of what they have read. By the end of a paragraph the concept is usually lost, because it has been so long since the paragraph had begun. By constantly re-reading, their ability to remember fades and they start doubting their ability to remember at all.

Their ability to read diminishes and the person re-reads more, then loses more trust in their memory and finally assumes that they don't understand what they are reading.

Let's say that on average you stop your eyes for one second. If you start stopping for half a second you will start reading 100% faster again. If you stop for one quarter of a second you will be reading 300% faster again. Do you remember that you could see the image of the planes in the video at one tenth of a second and the chick was flashed at one thirtieth of a second? So seeing a word at one quarter of a second is really possible.

3.1.2 More practice and the quantum leap

To help you understand the quantum leap you just made, I want to tell you a short story that illustrates what you've been through while practising to read with the metronome. You will be surprised to learn what happens inside your mind.

If you drive a car in your city or town, then you are driving most of the time at 30 mph (50 km/h); however, if you drive on the motorway, you gather speed until you are driving comfortably at 70 mph (110 km/h). Suddenly, you see a sign that indicates a small town ahead and you should slow down to 30 mph (50 km/h). You hit the brakes and slow down to a speed that seems to be slow enough to avoid getting flashed by the speed camera, which will ultimately result in a fine. Then you look down to check the speedometer and you realise that you are actually travelling much faster than 30 miles per hour (50 km/h).

It is very interesting how your brain gets used to the higher speed and then it doesn't want to slow down to levels that were acceptable before. You actually reset your mind at a faster speed.

It is important to know that:

When your mind is stretched to a new dimension it never goes back to its original shape.

Once you begin to speed up with your pointer and rhythm, you will start to feel comfortable at higher speeds. Naturally, you will begin to read faster. The mind starts to take in information using the right side of the brain; it is working so quickly that you don't have time to say the words in your mind. You are going quickly already.

Another secret of speed reading is that if you start reading at an even pace – let's say 500 WPM with the help of the metronome and the pointer – your comprehension will catch up.

This is the same principle of video games. You start playing and it feels very fast. Keep playing and your brain will get used to that speed because it is steady. Your response will enhance in a matter of minutes; an improvement which can be measured by your scores.

In the same way, your brain will give you the comprehension if you keep a steady pace for some time on one rhythm. The amount of time will depend on each individual person and also be variable according to the complexity of the material you are reading.

After continuous practice, you will read faster. The secret is to keep reading at a speed that is not too demanding, until your brain gives you that comprehension.

The magic happens because your brain works with feedback; whenever your eyes stop at the right place for the right amount of time you will have some comprehension. Your brain keeps track of the right strategy that yields the best results and will tend to repeat it. When this happens you will start understanding the text you are reading at 300, 500 or even 700 WPM. You should keep focused on the text but the actual process of developing is unconscious and relies on the coordination between brain, eyes and your pointer.

Be aware that different books will require an adequate reading speed, so try a few speeds to find the best one for a specific text.

Now decide which speed you liked the most and select the rhythm that will help you get consistent at one reading speed.

Keep playing the metronome to read this chapter.

Don't forget to use your pointer and you will keep improving as you read this book. Use the pointer with each of your hands and notice which one gives you the best understanding.

3.1.3 Important words can distract you

Did you know that words are not so important in face-to-face communication?

Research done by an expert in communication, Dr Albert Mehrabian, shows that only 7% of face-to-face communication is down to words. This is incredible because 55% of the message is expressed by facial expression, body language, eye contact and eventual touch. However, 38% of the content is delivered through the pace that we talk, volume, tone of voice, accent, pitch and much more.

Now you can understand why it is so difficult to focus your attention on reading material.

You read at the same speed that you talk and while you receive 100% of the message, the information given through words amounts to only 7% of the content. So only 7% of your effort is directed to the words and you can understand the whole conversation.

So, if you start reading a book at the speed that you talk, you would need only 7% of your energy to be able to understand the text. This way 93% of your attention needs to be redirected, otherwise your mind will start drifting away from the text and you will lose comprehension.

Your mind can process information very fast, but if you don't give it something interesting to focus on, it will disengage and get distracted. The problem is that you have too much mental power that is idle. Most people think it is difficult to speed up their reading because it will demand too much energy and focus, but in fact, they need to redirect their energy and comprehension will arise. It might sound like a paradox but it is not.

The important words hook you out of the text

Your mind will look at words that will trigger memories or random thoughts.

For example, let's say that you come across the word "trouble". If you read slowly, your mind can stop concentrating on the text and you start thinking about "trouble". Maybe your Tax Return or perhaps you will imagine how your client might react to a late delivery. You keep imagining things outside the book and it goes on and on.

The mind works with associations and will visually connect new ideas with others that lie in the unconscious mind.

Your brain loves speed

Our mind loves speed because fast is fun. As you learn to go faster you will start using your mind's eye to create the images described in the text. Your imagination will be activated, you will become more motivated and it is then that memory is created. It's not the words in the text but the ideas that you create in your mind that you will remember.

Another example of the brain working at speed would be playing a video game. The game has many levels and the higher the level you reach, the faster your brain has to think and the more exciting it gets.

With a bit of training you will develop quickly and will have more fun, either on computer games or while reading because your brain loves speed.

PART 2 - READING REALLY FAST

"You are never given a wish without also being given the power to make it come true."

Richard Bach

By reading this chapter you can expect to improve your reading speed by a further 10–40% while reading your books. Go for it!

Time to read this chapter

at 100 wpm	14 min
at 200 wpm	7 min
at 300 wpm	4 min
at 400 wpm	3 min
at 500 wpm	3 min
at 600 wpm	2 min
at 700 wpm	2 min
at 800 wpm	2 min
at 900 wpm	2 min
at 1000 wpm	1 min

3.2.1 Getting ready to read really fast

Now that you've read with the metronome and have been reading faster by using the pointer, you are ready to stretch yourself a little more and start developing your comprehension levels even further.

The first time you used the metronome sequence I was helping you to stretch your mind. Now we will be doing the same exercise with a twist. This time I will play three rhythms in sequence, i.e. from 30–50 beats per minute. I will also stop the beats after playing each one of them. You should keep reading at the same pace you were reading by moving your pointer at the same rhythm.

Once you reach 50 beats per minute (BPM), I will start going backwards and play 40, and then 30 BPM. I am sure that it will start to get easier because, after stretching your mind and reading at 500 WPM, your mind will become more active and you will read faster with less effort. Even if you didn't understand much at 40 or 50 BPM, your mind was working hard to gain some comprehension from the text and you will find it much easier to read at 30 or 40 BPM after reaching 50. I will play the beats to get you started on each rhythm and you keep the momentum going once I stop the beats.

Do you remember I said it feels very slow driving at 30 miles per hour shortly after driving at 70 miles per hour? The same principle will work when you read at 30 BPM just after reading at 50 BPM. Your brain will get stretched again and comprehension levels tend to increase. You can practise on any book of your choice.

The most important thing is to focus and to understand.

Please remember:

- To take a deep breath and relax while reading.

- Don't be anxious to learn everything at once.

- If you don't understand everything, it is OK, just keep up with the rhythm and comprehension will follow as a result.

Start playing a video from the second set of videos now! Go to the webpage below or open the Pro Metronome App and select the individual rhythms or create a bespoke sequence to play.

www.thespeedreadingcoach.com/audio

Select the right video for you and get ready with your pointer!

Karate Kid and you

Do you remember *The Karate Kid* film? If you've never seen it, I'll tell you the story in a few words.

Mr Miyagi, an old karate master, comes out of retirement when he is befriended by a teenager called Daniel, who is constantly being beaten by bullies at school. Daniel pleads with him to teach him karate in the hope that he can learn to defend himself.

Mr Miyagi agrees to teach him the art of self-defence but on condition that Daniel will commit to any request that he asks of him – without question. The training begins with Daniel having to sand the floor at Mr Miyagi's home, paint his fence and then wax his car.

Daniel, feeling frustrated of having to work and not having any karate lessons, complains to the master, who tells him that his training had already begun. To prove it, he threw a punch at Daniel and said with his commanding voice: "Wax on!"

The boy – obeying without thinking – blocked the punch with precision.

Daniel was learning karate while waxing the car because he was coordinating mind and body. In the same way, you will train your mind to see differently by using your pointer. Once your eyes learn how to move and stop over the lines, you will have good reading speed and comprehension. After some time practising, you will not need the pointer anymore. Your eyes should go where you want them to go and the pointer is a fundamental part of the training.

3.2.2 Choose a rhythm to practise and get good at it

The secret lies in going at a higher speed of, let's say, 400 WPM by following the rhythm of a metronome. If your normal reading speed is 200 WPM, you will be reading 100% faster with some help from your pointer.

In the first few minutes you try to coordinate the pointer though the rhythm and the comprehension will not be very good. Perhaps 10 minutes later you will get the hang of it and then you can see the words rushing in sequence at a faster pace.

Your brain loves a challenge and it performs very well when you try to play a video game for the first time. The improvement can be seen second after second. You learn the tricks, your mind gets sharper and your coordination becomes first class.

That is exactly what we will be doing. Make your eyes go fast and then your visual perception will start to kick in and you will then see more and understand it better because you are more focused. These are the results of switching the right side of the brain on. It will come alive when the task at hand is not suitable to the academic left side of the brain. The shift is made automatically.

Choose 400 WPM and keep the pace for some time. If you don't understand it, it is because your left side of the brain likes safety and will try to retreat to the traditional reading pace. But if you stay there, the left side will come out of its comfort zone and will be ready to give up. The right side is very holistic and understands the big picture and will take over the situation. This is the moment that the text starts to make sense. This is the big shift. You will start using your whole brain to read, instead of reading only with the left side of your brain.

You should read with purpose in mind or perhaps a question.

One that I like is this: How can I use this information?

Being in this frame of mind, you will be reading actively and not passively. Ask any question and you will activate the Reticular Activating System (RAS). If it were not for the RAS, you would become paralysed being faced by so many interesting things everywhere you go. The RAS make things easier. It helps you focus your attention.

So, choose one of the rhythms of the metronome and practise reading with it for half an hour. You can always switch it on and off while keeping the same pace. The comprehension will increase and you will become more confident to read faster and absorb the message from the text you are reading. Pick up another book to practise. After playing one of the video sequences to warm up, choose a rhythm to read for half an hour, and get good at it.

Have a good reading light

A good light is essential for good reading performance.

Look for options on the Internet that suit your needs. Light coming from over your shoulders can also be a good option if you are sitting in an armchair or even at your table.

Don't move your mouth while reading

If you mumble or whisper the words while reading, you should stop doing that because it holds you back in terms of speed and your reading will be limited.

By wiggling your tongue inside your mouth, you will hold yourself back in terms of performance, too.

Measure your improvement

You can test yourself again; let's see how fast you are going just by using the pointer and the metronome?

You can ask a friend to time you or use the timer on your phone.

Time yourself for exactly one minute while you read your book and keep track of your progress.

Chances are that you have improved a further 10–40% just by using a pointer and the metronome to help you get more focused and stop skipping back.

If you didn't improve much, don't worry because I will show you other exercises that might be more beneficial to you. Much more to come! So keep reading…

PART 3 - UNDERSTAND HOW TO SEE MORE

"The best effect of any book is that it excites the reader to self-activity."

Thomas Carlyle

If you read this chapter you can expect to improve your reading speed by a further 10–20%. You will see it happening easily.

Time to read this chapter

at 100 wpm	19 min
at 200 wpm	10 min
at 300 wpm	6 min
at 400 wpm	5 min
at 500 wpm	4 min
at 600 wpm	3 min
at 700 wpm	3 min
at 800 wpm	2 min
at 900 wpm	2 min
at 1000 wpm	2 min

3.3.1 Expanding your peripheral vision

The pointer will help you control your eyes

If you hold a pointer and make a spiral in the air in front of a person, their eyes will follow your pointer in a round swoop.

But now ask them to move their eyes in a spiral motion like before, but without the pointer as a guide, and their eyes will move in a jagged way, and not in a round spiral at all.

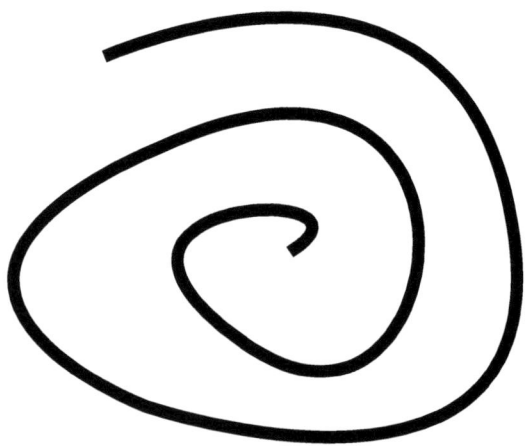

Using the pointer your eyes make a perfect spiral.

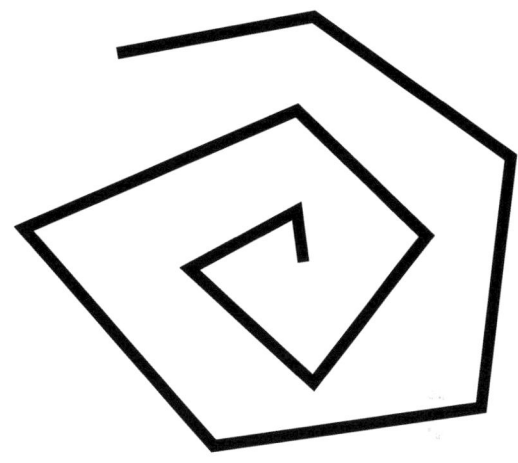

Without the pointer your eyes move around in a
jagged way.

Try this exercise with a friend and you will see that
without a pointer the eyes go places that they were
not supposed to go.

If you read with a pointer and train your eyes to read
faster, after some practice, your eyes will know where
to go and you won't need the pointer any more.

Expand your focal vision

I think that the way we are taught to read might have
a massive impact on the speed with which you feel
confident to read, perhaps for the rest of your life.

I believe that children should learn to read with the Analytic Phonics, also known as the Whole Word, approach instead of Synthetic Phonics, which teaches each letter and its sound before going into creating words.

Instead of absorbing two or three letters at a time, we can absorb four or five words at once and have good comprehension. Just expand your pericentral vision and read faster.

Having a scientific mind and based on a book called *Dyslexia Breakthrough* by Collin Corkum PhD and Jerri Girard-Corkum PhD, I found evidence that the way we are taught to read can activate only the very centre of the central focal area in the retina, which is called foveola. Some people will read slowly for the rest of their lives if they don't start to expand their focal vision. The earlier you learn how to expand your vision, the better.

As you can see in the image below, the foveola measures 0.35 millimetres in diameter, which is wide enough to focus clearly on four or five letters. If you read only with the foveola, which most of us do, your eyes will have to move far too many times to read. Some people might develop dyslexia as a result of this self-imposed limitation on the field of vision.

If you learn to read using the fovea, which includes the foveola and measures 1.5 millimeters, you will be able to read four or five words at once or five times more information than with the foveola alone. This way you can achieve a very good reading speed and read from 400–800 WPM.

The Parts and Functions of the Retina

 Central focal area (foveola)
– 0.35 millimetres in diameter
– Readability: 4–5 letters
– Average reading rate: 200 WPM

Pericentral focal area (fovea)
– 1.5 millimetres in diameter
– Readability: 4–5 words
– Average reading rate: 500 WPM

Peripheral vision area
Gives general information outside of the focal areas.

The exercises in this book will help you increase your focal vision, so you will become confident in reading fast and efficiently.

Please note that you should remember to start using your pointer half an inch (1 cm) after the beginning of the line and stop your pointer half an inch (1 cm) before the end of each line. Your peripheral vision will see the words at the extremities of the pages without having to go all the way. If you move your eyes from the beginning to the end of the page you will be using your active vision in the margins and this is a big waste!

The intention is to save fractions of seconds everywhere, so the result will be a great improvement.

Stop moving your head sideways

Some people move their heads sideways while reading one line of text. This is not necessary; your eyes can do the work and by not moving your head you save energy which can be used on comprehension. Can you imagine reading 100 pages of a book? You would be moving your head sideways 3,000 times. This really is a waste of energy.

Your head should be relaxed. Don't move it, just move your eyes.

This is ideal:

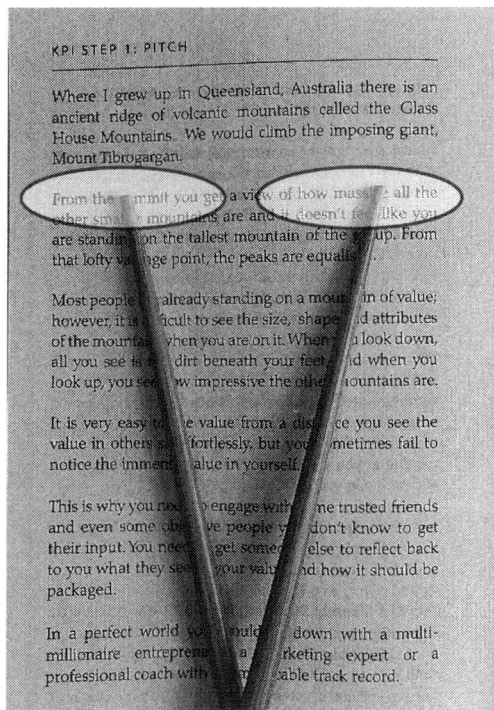

Start half an inch in and finish half an inch before the end.

This way you will expand your active vision.

You should avoid this:

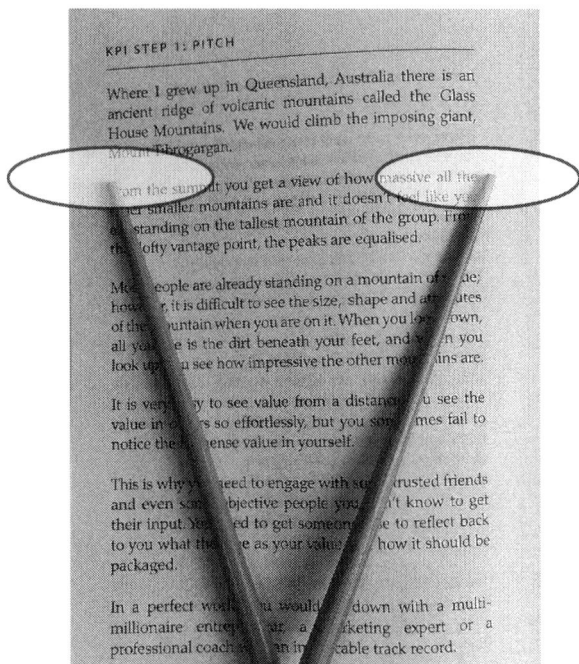

If you move your pointer through the whole line you will waste your active vision in the margins and miss the opportunity to expand your pericentral focal vision.

Practise eyerobics to develop your pericentral focal vision

Now that you've learned the basics you should keep reading the book using your pointer. Use it all the time and don't worry if people look at you using a pointer to read. They will actually be surprised to see you moving your pointer or pen down the page very quickly. If they ask what you are doing, you can just say that you are speed reading.

At this stage of the training you will be activating your brain to start expanding your focal vision to be able to see three, four, five or even six words every time you stop your eyes on a line of text. The easiest way to activate the brain is to move your eyes faster. With practice, your focal vision will naturally expand and you will start moving your eyes less while you learn more because your focal vision will have developed enough.

3.3.2 Computers can read and you can foresee the future

Bag of words on computer vision

There is a model in computer vision that is called "Bag of Words model". For example, "a good book" and "book good a" are the same under this model because it ignores the word order. This model can give you a lot of information about a text if you consider the Natural Language Processing. This means that computers can now read a text email and answer it without anyone looking at it.

Knowing that our brain is a sophisticated computer, I would like to introduce you to the "Bag of Letters model", which will give you great understanding of a text even if the letters of a word are jumbled up.

Read the text below with your pointer and don't linger on the words; your mental computer will give you the meaning of the text anyway. Some people have already noticed that they can read faster when the words are all jumbled up than when the words are written in the normal way. This is because it is very difficult to say a word in your mind if you can't say it out loud. This way, they end up avoiding the mental chatter and understand the text anyway. Strange but true.

Now it is your turn to try it for real. Get your pointer to help you move forward faster and read the text below.

This is relaly amzaing. Even thuogh msot of the wodrs beolw are jublmed up you can stlil undesrtand the txet. You can crack the cdoe if the fsirt and lsat lerttes are corrcet and will strat raeding fsater tahn you wuold raed the txet if it was wirtten in the tratidional way. It's diffiuclt to suond the wodrs isnide yuor haed as you raed the wodrs wrttien in a diffrenet way so you will strat reaidng fatser withuot noiticng.

This is graet becuase to be frnak I'm raelly bad at seplling.

The relevant message from this text is that you will have better comprehension by not focusing on individual words. The brain can process text more effectively if you can recognise a few words at a time.

Take a look at the word below. What does it mean?

Enitesin

You are probably puzzled because you've never seen this word before.

But if you read the word inside a sentence it becomes much easier.

Ablert Enitesin is accliemad as one of the gretaest and smertast siecntsits of all time.

If you have the bigger picture, all the words make more sense.

Grouping words together will help you read more effectively and you will increase your reading speed, too.

Now you can also understand that we read using mental templates that give you meaning inside a context. We think that the words are important but expressions are even more so.

If you can raed somehting and can geuss waht is coimng nxet you will be albe to undsertand the txet and strat foresieeng the futrue.

You can predict what the author will say

Sometimes you read new information; other times, the information is completely expected and you can then skip it without loss of comprehension or just use your pointer to speed up one or two lines.

The idea behind speed reading is to become flexible and go faster when you can and slower when you need to. So, you will probably be going a little faster now and a little slower when there is a need for it. If you start reading for longer, you might gain a second wind, which will give you a lot of comprehension whenever you get into a flow. You will probably forget you are reading and will have a smooth experience.

I was born in Brazil so my mother tongue is Portuguese, which is a language based on Latin like French, Spanish and Italian.

If you've ever learnt one of these languages, you might agree with me that Latin languages are more casual and you can say the same thing in many different ways. People in Britain are usually polite and you can almost predict the next few words they are going to say when talking to someone. The English language is full of expressions that will be repeated endlessly.

You can be reading in any language and you will always find those expressions that are full of meaning but can be read almost like one single word. Whenever you notice that a well-known expression is coming just jump a little ahead.

Pay attention to the fact that most authors keep using the same jargon of words and expressions, and this is called a literary style.

Finish the sentences and you will understand what I mean by predicting the future.

He didn't mind all the shouting. He was cool as a

_____

Stop that! Don't cry over spilled _____

Their shop is always busy and they are selling like hot _____

If you learn another area of knowledge you will then be faced with new words and expressions. Once you become familiarised with them, you can also speed read them. If you stumble upon a word two or three times, it is a sign that that word is quite important to learn; however, if it doesn't appear again just move ahead without regret.

You know more than you think so trust that you are following the train of thought and move ahead faster and with confidence.

Measure your improvement

You can test yourself again; let's see how fast you are going?

You can measure yourself by reading the next chapter for one minute.

You know what to do so keep track of your development.

Chances are, that by just avoiding the margins of the book, you will improve both your peripheral vision and your speed reading by a further 10–20%.

PART 4 - DEVELOPING FLEXIBILITY

"Action makes more fortune than caution."

Luc De Clapiers

When reading this chapter you can expect to improve your reading speed by a further 10–30%. For example, emails, Facebook posts, blogs and articles. So let's twist things around...

Time to read this chapter

at 100 wpm	13 min
at 200 wpm	7 min
at 300 wpm	4 min
at 400 wpm	3 min
at 500 wpm	3 min
at 600 wpm	2 min
at 700 wpm	2 min
at 800 wpm	2 min
at 900 wpm	1 min
at 1000 wpm	1 min

3.4.1 More practice using your awareness

You cannot expect to read faster if you don't train your eyes to go faster. This eye exercise will make the muscles of your eyes get fit very quickly, but you need to stretch the muscles to keep relaxed and strong.

Now I will show you how to relax your eyes and you can do it in two different ways:

If you close your eyes and squeeze them together for a few seconds, you will release the tension from them. So, now blink your eyes a couple of times, squeezing them together or open them very wide, look up, down and sideways. Do it a few times and feel your eyes relaxing.

The other way is to rub your hands together and when you feel the heat on your palms, cover your eyes with your hands to energise them. It feels good.

This is how to move your eyes down the page

Once your brain starts to process information faster, the eyes will start to move less and will see more, due to the increase in focal vision.

In the example below I've underlined the area that you would be covering with your eyes when you start reading new text or start a new chapter or article.

The idea is to create a smooth transition from the traditional way of reading into speed reading.

You can observe that the eyes would cover the first few lines in the traditional way so you can get the first impressions of the passage very clearly.

As you become familiar with the text, you will start speeding up.

Read the text below, concentrating on reading only what is underlined and see if you can understand the text.

If you go from the beginning of the line until the end you would waste your peripheral vision on the margins.

If you pay attention to the text you can figure out if there is something interesting to come or something that you can foresee. A lot of the time the author is waffling – even repeating – therefore if you got the message you will even be able to skip a few lines because you can see what is coming next.

You will learn that you will gather speed as you keep reading and get into flow. As you move forward you will feel more confident in not reading all the lines and also will start expanding your peripheral vision even more.

Practice with your pointer will give you more control and you will build your confidence by getting the message.

Great! You are doing very well and just by learning these principles you will be reading faster automatically.

Parallel Reality

Now the big surprise. Whenever you keep reading and start to go above 500 WPM, your eyes will stop moving sideways as much. Instead of both eyes converging to the same words, they will start to move along the line in a parallel gaze, which means that each eye will see different words and your brain will integrate the message in an instant.

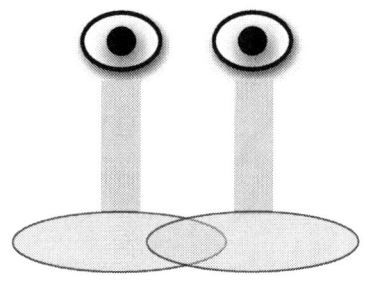

Reading by converging
150-500 WPM

Reading by looking parallel
500-1,000+ WPM

The following lines show the eye movement of someone reading at 500 or 700 WPM. Notice that the underlined words on the left will be covered by the left eye and the words underlined on the right will be covered by the right eye. This is just a schematic representation of the eye movement. You will start to go down the page quite quickly once you start to read faster and your focal vision will expand even more.

At the beginning of the practice you were making both eyes move along the lines very fast and the intention was to activate your brain to receive information faster. Once it gets used to this new stream of information it will be natural that they start gazing at the lines in a parallel motion. You won't need to move your eyes sideways so much and will naturally develop speed by seeing more while moving your eyes less. This is really incredible and this is the reason I call this stage "Parallel Reality".

To get you really confident, to read faster you should practise reading newspaper and magazine

They are great because the narrow columns are much easier to read than long ones. Articles have a catchy headline and you can get the information you need quite quickly if you feel secure to plough along. If by the end of the article you feel that you didn't get the main points, then just read the article again at a good speed. It is also very reassuring to read an article again because only then do you realise that you understood most of the text. It's harder to retrieve information than recognise it by reading for the second time.

If you concentrate on the centre of the line, you will find the words easier to define. Don't get scared if you start seeing two or three lines at a time and understand the message in narrow columns.

You start by reading the first few lines from beginning to end at a slower pace. Then you stop covering the margins and start to go faster. Whenever you follow the train of thought, keep connected to the main message. Be flexible to skip, scan and skim the text aiming to get the core message. As you get the message you feel more confident to go faster in the next article.

Sometimes you will be moving your eyes in a slight zigzag motion down the page. If you know a little bit about the subject you are reading you will find the new information amongst the padding. As you get more confident you might start to see two lines at a time and even skip a few lines that have information that is not relevant. I'm trying to show that each eye will stop in a slightly different place.

Practising free flow

Now let's practise again. This time things will start to get easier.

You will choose the rhythm that you think you are more comfortable reading and you will read with it for 30 minutes.

If you feel like changing tracks halfway, that's fine.

It is also good practice to play one rhythm for some time and stop the beats but keep reading on. After a while the beats will be inside your head. It is good to make the transition between having the beats on and off and keep the reading in a new flow.

This is like the stabilisers on your bike when you were a child or the person holding the bike from behind while you were trying to balance. It is a happy surprise to notice that you are riding without any help but at the same time you felt supported.

Please remember to go forward and avoid going back to re-read a line all the time. Try to go until the end of the page before deciding to go back. If you miss something it is OK, try to pay more attention and you might find out that the important information will appear again somewhere else before the end of the page.

Get ready and practise on another book for about 30 minutes before reading the next chapter.

PART 5 - BOUNCE AROUND AND BE IN CHARGE

"Imagination grows by exercise and contrary to common belief, is more powerful in the mature than in the young."

Paul McCartney

You are in charge. Read this chapter and improve your reading speed by a further 10–30%.

Time to read this chapter

at 100 wpm	21 min
at 200 wpm	11 min
at 300 wpm	7 min
at 400 wpm	5 min
at 500 wpm	4 min
at 600 wpm	4 min
at 700 wpm	3 min
at 800 wpm	3 min
at 900 wpm	2 min
at 1000 wpm	2 min

3.5.1 Be in charge without the metronome

The Bouncing Style

If you don't use the metronome support you can use the "Bouncing Style".

Knowing that your eyes follow movement you can move your pointer across the lines and stop two or three times over each line and develop your reading ability. This way your peripheral vision expands and you give yourself a pace to read that will push you to improve over and over again.

It is enough to stop fewer times and get the big picture, see the important words and move on. Your mind will give you enough detail so you can understand the content.

Try it now; keep reading this book until the next chapter and practise by using a pointer or a pen. Stop two or three times on each line and remember not to linger on each stop too long. Your eyes can see an image in less than one hundredth of a second so trust yourself and the comprehension will follow. Dare to go faster... and miracles will happen.

START BOUNCING NOW!

3.5.2 Set yourself a realistic routine and great goals

Success in a new ability comes when learned properly, practised daily and used in your everyday life.

If you commit yourself to practise the techniques you've learnt and read at least 15 pages per day, you will change your life for the better.

Remember, it's not enough to "learn" how to speed read; you need to practise all the steps to master it! You can improve from 20% to more than 100% by practice alone!!!

With your best intention you plan to read regularly and set yourself a target of 15 pages a day, but the chances are that you will start strong but will give up after a month or even less. New Year's resolutions work the same way.

What I want to teach you is a system that will keep you motivated because you will always reach your target, every single day, and with almost no effort!

Choose a book that you really want to read to start using this system.

Using the *Mini Max Target*

I love the system that I've named *Mini Max Target,* which will help you reach your goals and establish a new routine ... avoiding failure from the start.

I recommend you to set a target to read 15 pages of a book every single day!

This may seem reasonable but there will be some days that you will not have the time to read the 15 pages. A couple of days like this and you break your routine, and before you know it, you've stopped your daily reading habit all together. This happens because you break the chain of events that would stay strong if your life was boring and uneventful; but it is not. You need to deal with unexpected events that will take you off track. For example, you are invited to a party and so you don't have the time to read your 15 pages. You decide that to keep on track you will read 30 pages the following day to compensate but then it feels overwhelming and you don't read anything again. This is the beginning of the end! Don't get trapped in a commitment that is too difficult to keep up. Give yourself a little flexibility and it will be much easier to stay on track!

I would like you to think that you have a *Mini Target* that would be very easy to achieve, which is just one page a day. It's going to be very easy for you to keep your commitment now! You can read one page in bed, commuting to work, during your lunch break, or you can even keep a book in the bathroom for a quick read.

The good thing is that some days you will start with the one-page challenge and before you know it, you will have read 15 pages, which is your real target. Other days you will be really engrossed with the book and read 30 pages; this is the *Max Target*!

What's important is that your target is easily achievable and it will lead you naturally to the next target, and with little effort on your part.

So, decide today to pick up a book and start the *Mini Max Target* to help you create the habit of reading books.

You can track your progress by using your diary. Mark on each day how many pages you've read and you will become more motivated to read more and more every day of your life.

The example above is my personal *Mini Max Target*. You can do the same as me or choose the target that feels right for you.

Stop using the pointer

At this stage you can stop using the pointer, while maintaining the bouncing technique, using only your eyes. You will get the hang of it and your eyes will have an internal rhythm to follow. Your peripheral vision will expand and you will get to a new comfort zone in no time at all.

The bouncing technique works very well for books, but it is especially good for reading small chunks of text like emails or small articles. Practise for yourself and measure the results!

A new strategy to bounce

After spending some time practising, you will see that you don't need to point two or three times but just once on each line and go down in a slight zigzag.

The easy way to experience this is by reading an article in the newspaper. The headlines are usually very catchy phrases that leave a question in the air. This is the reason you read the article, to find the missing link or a specific piece of information. So, now get the paper or a magazine and try to read by tapping your pointer just once on each line. The columns are narrow and in no time, you will be able to see two or three lines at once, perhaps more than that. You can also use this technique on books.

Now start reading with or without your pointer. Apply the techniques described above and go on a zigzag. I believe that you will be surprised to understand the text because now your RAS will make all the relevant information stand out.

The text below is simulating a column of a newspaper or magazine to make you understand how easy this technique is.

Start the zigzag now!

3.e.3 There is a lot of repetition in books as you can see by now

I believe that we talk a lot to say very little, and when you are reading a non-fiction book you will realise that 20–50% of the information is just padding and repetition. Don't worry too much if you miss a sentence because it is very likely that it will come back again in the conversation.

I found this quote from Mark Twain that is very insightful:

"I am sorry to write such a long letter. I didn't have time to write a short one."

I've been very interested in producing book summaries and I found out that the English language is redundant for up to 70% of the time, according to Dr John Davies, who leads the Semantic Technology research group at BT and developed a software to summarise text called *Prosum*. This significant figure means that we repeat ourselves all the time. Exactly like I've just done now. I said redundant and I guess you know what redundant means, however I've explained it and written: "This means that we repeat ourselves all the time." Do you realise how much repetition there is out there and we don't notice it is just repetition?

Now I'll repeat myself for the third time and I'll give you an example:

"The little boy went to school in the morning."

It seems a simple sentence but notice that when I say boy it almost implies that a boy must be little, little boys go to school and, apparently, in England if they don't, their parents can go to jail. And I don't even need to mention that the school is in the morning. Got it?

So, as you can see, I kept repeating myself in different ways and we do it all the time; so keep reading forward and notice how much the same ideas are repeated.

My intention in this small chapter was to repeat a few concepts I find interesting and useful. Repeating so you will remember how much people repeat themselves while talking and writing.

Read faster to get the big picture by seeing what matters and being able to skip, scan or skim what is just padding.

3.5.4 Stop to think and you will remember more

To help you perform better and remember more of what you read, I would like to emphasise how important it is to stop and think about what you've just read. This is when memory is created.

After reading a few paragraphs that have good content, stop for a moment and try to remember the most important information there. Stop again at the end of a chapter and visualise what is important or essential; also remember some details.

This is the moment that you will be creating a book inside your head because instead of reading it passively, you will be recreating the entire story in your mind in a few seconds, and by doing so, you will keep that information alive and dynamic.

So, stop now and think for a few seconds; try to remember the most important information from this book. What was more relevant to you? Make the effort and try to remember, as this is when your memory will be created. Do it now!

Stop and think after a chapter, before and after a class or an important conversation. When you stop and think about the new information, you reorganise ideas in an order that is particular to you, filtered by your own experience.

To begin with, you will have to make a conscious effort, but soon the brain will start to retrieve information on autopilot.

If you are engaged in formal education or taking a course, pay attention to the teacher and when the lesson is over, try to remember what was important. At the beginning of a new lesson, try to remember what was discussed in the previous one. It will take you just a few seconds to retrieve the information but the results will surprise you. Your memory will get better and better! You can always take notes, too.

Finally, as you are reading words, these words will help you create images. It is also important to focus on these images and add more colour, more detail and motion to them. Instead of thinking in pictures, try to think like you are watching a film. You will remember these moving images you create more vividly than the words written on the page. Practise using Mind Maps and you will integrate the left side and right side of the brain with obvious improvement on your memory.

Talking is another way to improve your memory. Talk about what you've just learned and you will make all that information become yours. If you have the chance to teach, the retention will be even better.

Another helpful technique

As you experiment reading without the pointer, you can use a piece of paper or card as you work your way down the page.

Please look at the following pictures.

Showing text from underneath.

Covering text from the top.

Read the next chapter without the pointer. Instead, use a piece of paper or a card to help you to read faster. Just try; if you like it, you can do it more often.

Measure your improvement

You can test yourself again and let's see how fast you are going.

You can measure it yourself reading the next chapter with or without the pointer for one minute.

PART 6 - BREAKING AN OLD HABIT

"In a time of turbulence and change, it is more true than ever that knowledge is power."

John F. Kennedy

If you read this chapter you can expect to improve your reading speed by a further 10–30%. If you are a very rational thinker and feel attached to the sound of the words, this information can be very liberating.

Time to read this chapter

at 100 wpm	18 min
at 200 wpm	9 min
at 300 wpm	6 min
at 400 wpm	4 min
at 500 wpm	3 min
at 600 wpm	3 min
at 700 wpm	2 min
at 800 wpm	2 min
at 900 wpm	2 min
at 1000 wpm	2 min

3.6.1 You can silence the inner voice

A picture is worth a thousand words

You know that if you look at a picture you understand the image without having to describe all the details in words. You also know that a picture is worth a thousand words. This is very true because the left side of the brain deals with words by being sequential and linear while the right side appreciates and understands whole images.

Now look at a word like it was an image; a self-contained package of information that you don't need to read but you will recognise as a message. Logos make you aware of the cost of any purchase. In the same way every word is a logo or icon. You can understand it just by looking at it instead of reading them from beginning to end.

Silence the inner voice

The way to silence your inner voice is to look at words not as sound units, but image units that make sense and can communicate ideas.

For silent readers, they make micro-movements with their tongue as they associate the sound of their own voice. To break this habit you can apply pressure on your tongue with your teeth.

Clamp your tongue lightly with your front teeth and keep reading!

It is very interesting to notice that some people feel very strange and awkward by not having the freedom to move their tongue freely while reading. This is very enlightening because they will break an old and engrained habit. As soon as your brain starts to disconnect with the imaginary sound and the need to wiggle your tongue inside your mouth, you will naturally start to read faster. I bet you are experiencing this already.

Reduce the noise inside your head and switch off your imaginary voice

Firstly, your imaginary voice will never go away completely. Your voice is your friend and your identity; it will be with you whenever you start thinking to yourself, writing something or even when you read a headline or a small article. But there are ways to make the voice subside while reading. The voice will come and go and this exercise will help you get more detached from the need to speak words inside your head to be able to understand their meaning.

There is a way to silence the voice. The role of the voice is not necessary to understand the text – it is just a long, established habit.

Today you will break the pattern of associating comprehension with the sound of your imaginary voice.

Some people that can *touch type* can already write without the sound of their voice because they end up typing faster than they can talk. This is proof that you can process written information faster than the speed of your normal reading.

So, now you will try something a little different...

It will be fun and it will bring you amazing results. Your mind will start digesting knowledge without the sound.

To stop your imaginary voice saying the words inside your mind, you will create another voice that will be humming a sound like ma, ma, ma, ma, inside your head, or out loud if you are alone in the room. You will not be able to say two things at once so your imaginary voice that says the words from the text will start to subside in order for you to keep repeating a syllable. Comprehension will develop as you practise because you will start to understand the message visually.

This exercise will help you develop this detachment while you say something like ma, ma, ma, ma, and keep reading. As you can imagine, it is difficult to understand the text but your brain is cleverer than you think.

Keep reading this chapter and saying ma, ma, ma.

Start doing it now! Start humming!

Your attention will start to split and you will begin to feel confident, saying something that is not in the text you are reading, while understanding the text. You will start improving your reading speed straight away; just persist on the training reading while saying ma, ma, ma, for a few pages of a book. This is a great warm up. Once you start feeling lighter from having to say all the words inside your head it is time to gather speed again on your book. Get your pointer, stop humming and start reading faster than before.

Your brain will start to feel free from the imaginary sound of the words you read. You are not really sounding the words out inside your head, you are just imagining doing so and you distort that voice because it is not real and can be silenced with a bit of training. I think that it is a great idea practising to read while repeating the same sound to trick your mind.

It's not as difficult as it appears. Just relax, take a deep breath and keep reading slowly for good comprehension while you keep humming. To get the best results I would recommend that you read two pages a day while humming for about two weeks.

Your brain will get detached from the sound of the words and go much faster whenever you read and push your speed.

Let me tell you a short story to illustrate the power of humming while reading.

Years ago I used to practise Thai Boxing. If you've never seen it before I can explain how it works. It's like normal boxing but you can also use your legs to kick the opponent's body or head. It is a very fast-paced martial art and it is very fun too. One of the exercises we used to do was to kick a punch bag or have a buddy to throw some high kicks. Before starting, we would wrap lead pouches around our ankles. We would go and kick those bags until we got tired and then we would take the lead pouches away and I felt that I could fly like a bird. I still remember that my first experience of walking the walls was immediately after exercising with the pouches. I'd run towards the wall and try to walk on it. To my surprise, I gave three solid steps on the wall. It was an incredible experience! I was faster and more powerful than ever. What felt like weighing me down was in fact liberating me.

The same will happen to you if you weigh yourself down a little by humming. It feels like it is holding you back but in fact it will help you feel liberated. When you stop humming and start reading for speed you will feel so much lighter to go faster. Try it for a few minutes and the results will start to appear immediately.

Practise repeating a sound while reading and then stop and just go for speed. Put the metronome on and select a track, and then give it a try. If it works, then keep working with it; if not, you can always change the pace and go slower or faster. Whatever suits you best.

Stop humming ma, ma, ma.

Now I want you to try an extension of the ma, ma, ma exercise.

While reading, start counting numbers from one to 100 inside your head. This seems a little difficult but it is not.

It will definitely break the old pattern of associating comprehension with the imaginary sound of your voice.

Keep reading and counting until the end of this chapter and you will benefit from getting more detached from your voice and you will become faster as a result.

If you are counting and halfway through you forget where you were, just take an educated guess and then continue with the process. It doesn't matter providing you keep reading and counting. Once you get to 100, return to the beginning of your count and continue reading.

Start doing it now!

Keep reading and counting in your head from one to 100

Listen to music or watch TV while reading

This is another way of getting detached from the little voice that torments our minds. If you listen to music while reading, you might pay attention to music and it will help you silence your little voice and then you get to read faster with less effort.

Try different kinds of music and, if it works for you, do more of it.

There is a Bulgarian psychotherapist called Georgi Lozanov, who developed a teaching method to learn languages where classical Baroque music is played while you learn. This method can accelerate the speed of learning by two or three times. The point I'm making is that from this study, many researchers found that a selection of tracks from *Mozart* have a relaxing effect that can aid the brain to study and learn. It is now very common to talk about the *Mozart Effect,* which is the result of research that suggests that a selection of *Mozart's* music can, in fact, improve mental performance. You can find more information about it and download the music if you Google it. Try it for yourself and see the results.

Some people can also read while watching the television. Maybe you can give it a proper trial. You might focus on the book and at some point you flick your attention to the TV and then go back to the book. I think that becoming more versatile and developing attention while under noise pollution is a great skill to master. It will help develop your focus. An advantage of reading in front of the TV is that you will be less likely to become hypnotised with what you are viewing and will therefore pay more attention to what you are reading. I also like browsing on my iPad or iPhone while watching TV at a friend's house.

PART 7 - SAYING THE KEYWORDS AND REMEMBERING THEM

"The important thing is not being afraid to take a chance. Remember, the greatest failure is to not try."

Debbi Fields

If you read on, you can expect to improve your reading speed even further. You will start to get drawn to the important information and will remember more of what really matters.

Time to read this chapter

at 100 wpm	28 min
at 200 wpm	14 min
at 300 wpm	9 min
at 400 wpm	7 min
at 500 wpm	5 min
at 600 wpm	5 min
at 700 wpm	4 min
at 800 wpm	3 min
at 900 wpm	3 min
at 1000 wpm	3 min

3.7.1 Selecting the keywords to sub-vocalise

Saying the keywords in your mind can help you, too

Another way of tricking the mind is by reading and saying (in your mind) the keywords – or the bigger words – without the need to worry about saying linking words like "and", "the", "or", "but" or any other small word. Just focus and look out for the keywords to grasp the meaning of the sentence. You probably remember that this was one of the first ideas I shared with you to help you read faster, but only now you have the understanding to use this technique effectively.

Initially, you will make a conscious effort to instinctively distinguish the keywords in the text. The Reticular Activating System will kick in and start to give it to you. In next to no time you will be automatically finding the message because the keywords will start to stand out from the page to give you the message you are after.

Read actively looking for connections and important messages. Sound out the important words inside your head – usually the big words – and continue to practise.

Start saying the keywords in your mind until the end of the chapter.

Now be aware that you will be reading quickly for a few minutes; while reading complex material, you may slow down to allow yourself to grasp the subject. That's OK, you can go faster and slower. Just use your pointer as much as you can and keep pushing your boundaries and become more flexible.

After doing this exercise, try to read without using the pointer. You will be surprised by how much the words begin to stand out, which will give you a clearer understanding of the overall text.

3.7.2 Sub-vocalise only half of the keywords

Now that you are aware that you can understand a text well without sub-vocalizing the linking words, I will present you with another challenge.

I want you to say half or just part of the keywords on purpose and understand the meaning of the text. It feels like you are mumbling the words to yourself rather than reading them completely.

You will start saving time on every word. It is fractions of seconds saved all the time. This will result in having a substantial improvement on your reading speed and will stretch your comfort zone to become more flexible while reading different kinds of material.

Ensure you are aware that you are saying the words inside your mind; make every effort to say only part of the important words and you will start developing an excellent strategy that will become second nature in no time at all.

3.7.3 Developing your memory

Marking your books can help you to remember

I know that a lot of people are against writing or marking books and I respect that, however, my books are full of marks in pencil or even pen, post-its or highlighted in yellow. This way I pay more attention to what is really important.

Another use of a pencil is to mark exactly the last line you've read whenever you have a break, or you are interrupted by a phone call or someone enters the room and starts telling you something.

If you don't mark the last line you read, you will inevitably close your book, slipping in a book mark between two pages and by doing so, create a problem the next time you revisit the book. It is likely that you will begin reading from the opening passage on the left hand page and therefore re-read part of the text.

Psychologically you end up not wanting to go back to the book because you feel that you are a bit lost there. You've probably had the experience of watching a movie and stopping it halfway through only to find yourself searching for the last bit you remember watching before falling asleep. It is very frustrating to keep rewinding and fast forwarding until you find the place that you know you already watched for sure.

The same happens whenever you read a book. Marking the last line you read will let you get back on track straightaway. It's like a pause button. So, whenever you go back to the book you don't waste time re-reading one whole page that you already read. If you know where you've finished at the last reading session, you are more likely to start reading again sooner. If you don't want your book having lots of little marks in the margins, then you can always use a rubber whenever you start reading again from that point onwards. You can use a post-it or a bookmark that you insert from the side of the page like an arrow and it tells you exactly which line you read last.

You should skip back to re-read when you find something outstanding. Be on the lookout for a great idea.

I know that at the beginning of the book I was advising you to avoid skipping back if you don't understand something.

Here's the surprise!

I would recommend that you skip back to re-read a passage if you see something that seems important, because you want to mark or highlight those lines and make that information stronger in your brain. Use a pencil or even a pen to mark the book. If you don't like writing in your book, then just use a post-it note. Making notes can be useful so that you can find that nugget of information at a later date.

A tech savvy alternative to highlighting or marking your books is the App called TextGrabber. Take pictures of text, select the lines you want to keep and it will convert the pictures into editable text. It also instantly translates restaurant menus, magazines or any text into your native language.

Your books will become a powerful reference if you start marking them. In the same way you create files on your computer to gather similar information, you can start marking your books and writing down on the side the point of reference. This way you will start to recognise that whatever is higher on your values system will start to appear more in the margins of your books.

For example, my books have marks with words like "Memory" or "For Book 2" or "Focus" or other things that can be useful at a later date. Sometimes, I forget what I've marked and I need to flick through the book quickly to find the good stuff. But many times if something is important and I've put a post-it there with a title or have even written a paragraph about it on the post-it note, I'm very likely to remember the information by heart.

By doing that, I get more out of the books or documents I read, especially if I write something on the spot because then I'm creating information in my own right. You can do the same.

Some people don't know what their passion in life is but if they start reading and marking their books, the passion will start to become more apparent. Well, it certainly helps me to find what I want to get more involved with.

Just the act of marking the book sends a strong message to your brain, reinforcing the need to remember that particular topic.

By having a pencil and being willing to find something interesting in the book, you become an active reader instead of a passive reader. It will direct your attention to what you're reading and activate the RAS to find things that are relevant.

Just stop and think about what was said in the book in your own words or recollect your thoughts, images, feelings, whatever works for you. By thinking about it you develop extreme focus and it is not difficult to do so. Just think for five seconds to enhance the possibility of remembering something and things will stick there for longer. That's my experience.

Detectives use torches to focus their attention

Have you ever noticed that in detective films detectives constantly walk into a crime scene and switch their torches on even if the place is well lit? If the place is dark they usually avoid turning the lights on. Why is that?

It is easier to see the detail if you have a smaller area to cover. The flashlight helps them to get focused; it guides the detective's eyes to what might be important. If you have too much to take in, your mind gets overloaded and you can miss important details.

The same will happen when you use a pencil or a pen. Your RAS will be turned on and you will find more relevant information because there is a purpose to your reading.

If you are reading on your iPad or Kindle, it's easy to mark the book and make notes too.

So, if you flick through the book you will find little drawings and keywords that will trigger your memory. This way you are active, searching for meaning and finding it. If you don't search for meaning you will not find it so easily.

I would like to recommend an App, which is great for gathering information on subjects that you may be interested in. It's called *Evernote*. I use it a lot.

A great way to take notes

There is a method for note-taking that is called *Cornell Notes*, which is very simple and makes your mind pick up the key concepts of a lecture or book, and helps you to develop your memory.

The steps to take notes are:

Divide the paper into three sections: From the top draw two lines one inch apart and a line two inches from the bottom. Draw another line two inches from the left of the paper like the drawing on the next page:

Note-taking for:	Date:
Purpose to read:	
Note-taking	Questions & Keywords
Summary	

In the left column you will take your notes, which include the main ideas of the text or lecture and you can use bullet points, short sentences and drawings. In the right column you can write the purpose of reading that book or the main questions you might have about it. Write also the keywords or key concepts from the message. Drawings are always welcome.

After taking your notes I recommend that you use the space at the bottom of the page to write a brief summary of the material you've been studying. This helps your mind integrate the new ideas in an active way.

Mind Maps can help you think clearer

Mind Maps are a great invention of Tony Buzan. I would recommend that you learn how to use them, as you will start to develop the right side of your brain and find new ways to memorise ideas.

Tony says that Mind Maps are great to make notes or summarise concepts. This is because we communicate mostly with key concepts and you can encapsulate them inside bubbles, draw colourful images inside, and write just the keywords on the lines that link each bubble.

He also says that we waste 90% of our time while making notes because we use far too many words which could be better represented by a little drawing.

The basic Mind Mapping Laws are:

•   Use a plain sheet of paper in landscape position. In the centre of the paper draw a colourful image that represents the title of the Mind Map.

•   Create images throughout your Mind Map.

•   Use printed words on the lines that connect every thought bubble.

•   Your drawings can be very basic and what really counts is the energy you use to create something out of the ordinary; strange details or colours will aid your memory.

Recently I was preparing myself to give a talk and I created a Mind Map. I could recall the Mind Map and knew what was next in my presentation. Below is a little example of it.

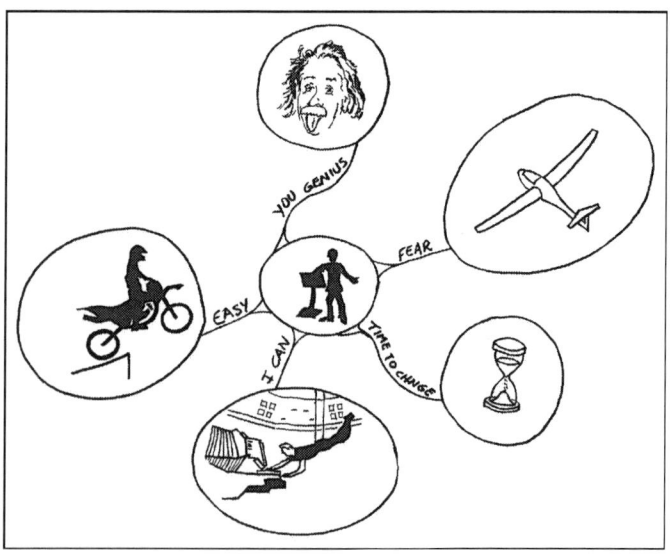

You can use Mind Maps for lectures to show how ideas and plans connect while explaining them. If you are running a meeting you can also apply the same concepts to present an idea or plan and invite people to contribute and visually fit new ideas in the Mind Map. This helps to reduce redundant ideas and calm people down when they see their idea clearly in the right place.

If you try to create a Mind Map at a meeting you will also have a clear summary about what took place. There are many types of software that can help you create a good Mind Map.

I think that by becoming more playful you will develop your creativity and have things done in less time. I like using Mind Maps and would recommend that you buy Tony's book. You will find more information on the website below.

www.imindmap.com

I'm getting more and more digital but I still like to keep a small notebook in my pocket to take notes. I believe that everything you focus on grows, so just by carrying a notebook I'm focused on having new ideas, and therefore they will come to me.

The curve of forgetfulness

We will remember things that are higher in our value system, but as a general rule, I have some figures that illustrate, in a general sense, the *Cone of Learning* from Edgar Dale:

Average retention rates according to teaching methods

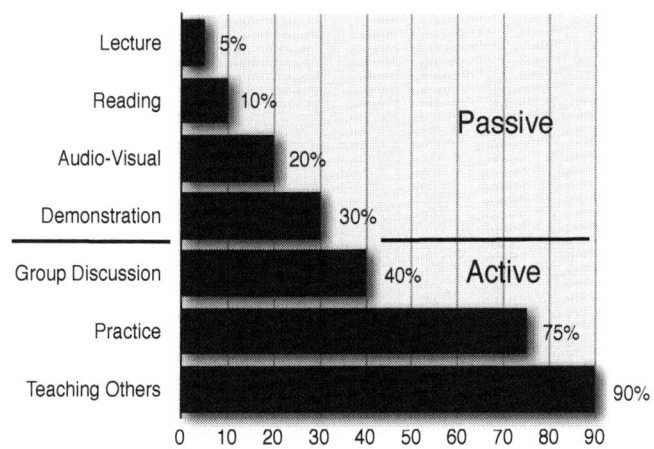

Mr Dale also arrived at some conclusions about the residual memory, and he says that after two weeks we remember:

10% of what we read;
20% of what we hear;
30% of what we see;
50% of what we see and hear;
70% of what we say,
and 90% of what we see, hear, say and do.

Therefore, the secret to successful retention is to combine seeing, hearing, saying and doing and one of the best ways to do this is by using your imagination to see the information with your mind's eye, say the information to yourself or to others and take action using the new information. If you make it fun it will be even better...

The following graph shows you how we forget things the moment we stop receiving any information and you will have perhaps 5% residual memory after a month.

If you think about the subject again after one hour, you will create memory just by trying to remember what you've learnt, and this could improve your residual memory by 5% after a month.

By writing a blog after one day has passed you will be actively creating content that will reinforce your capacity of remembering that information, which might add another 5% residual memory after a month.

If you decide to give a short talk about the subject after a week you will probably enhance your residual memory by another 5%.

Every time you learn something you tend to forget details and the core information will leave a residual memory after a month, a year or even 40 years. Just by trying to remember you will remember more. That's exactly what you can see in the graph. Every time you try to remember something in any shape or form you go to another level of abstraction and create your own memory. I think this is amazing!

The more you think about it, you create more memory that will become more easily available.

The increase of residual memory graph

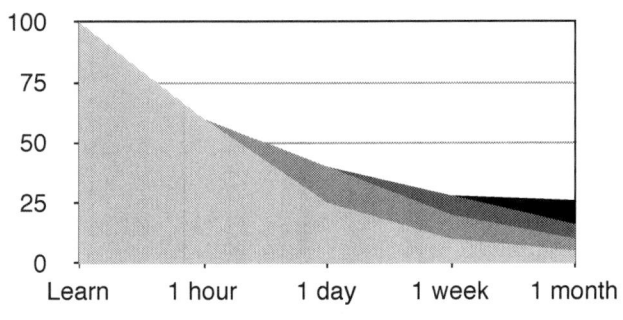

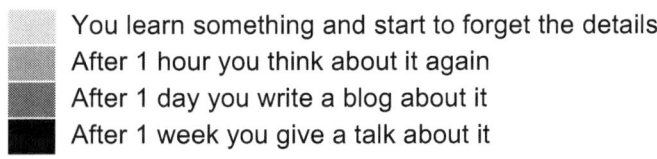

You learn something and start to forget the details
After 1 hour you think about it again
After 1 day you write a blog about it
After 1 week you give a talk about it

We are constantly being bombarded by new information and get distracted. By deciding to remember something you have learnt, you will become more focused and will also enhance your power of imagination, which will help you create new solutions for the problems that you will face in the future.

Memory is stored in the unconscious mind; so trust your unconscious to give you the answers, trust in your judgement and use the information you are receiving to remember more of what you read.

I believe that you should teach what you want to learn. To learn any subject takes years and if you are committed to sharing the wisdom you've received you will develop faster. As a result, you will be learning much more in less time.

Knowing that you might be sharing your knowledge in the near future will also help you because every time you read something interesting, you will be thinking about the main points of the book now that you have a bigger purpose to learn. This way you will be focusing more on the text you are reading and will remember more as a result.

What about writing a blog? It is easy to do and I think that it would be beneficial for you to do so. To get started, search for a blog on Google that helps people "create a blog". Create a profile for yourself and start writing.

I know it can feel threatening to expose yourself, but nowadays we can make a lot of money just by giving advice. So, if you want to be found and start to raise your reputation, you need to be found on Google. By writing a blog, your confidence will increase and you will remember what you've written. Every time you express an idea you will be helping yourself to remember more of what is important to you. You can start by writing a comment on someone else's blog, and whenever you feel a little more confident, you can then write your own. You will start to leave a legacy by writing some words that will be available on the internet forever.

Before you keep reading, stop and think about what you have learnt so far from this chapter. This way you will create memory as it is your own take on information.

DEVELOP YOUR PASSION FOR BOOKS

"Whatever your wildest dreams may be, they only scratch the surface of what is possible."

Michael Berg

Read on and improve your reading speed by a further 10–30% or more. You will become more inspired to read, and therefore you will apply your knowledge to settle down in a new comfort zone.

Time to read this chapter

at 100 wpm	18 min
at 200 wpm	9 min
at 300 wpm	5 min
at 400 wpm	5 min
at 500 wpm	4 min
at 600 wpm	3 min
at 700 wpm	3 min
at 800 wpm	2 min
at 900 wpm	2 min
at 1000 wpm	2 min

4.1 The final exercise

I've got an exercise that you might want to try while reading this or another book of your choice. Now you will be playing one of the ON/OFF video sequences that go up and down. For example you can choose to play it from 40 beats per minute (BPM) until 60, and then you go back until you read again at 40 BPM. Alternatively, you can play other variations available.

This final exercise requires you to start using the pointer every time you start a new rhythm. After about 15 seconds, you should stop using the pointer and see if you can keep up with the pace and comprehension. This should be done while listening to the metronome, and when I stop the metronome you will keep reading in silence at the same pace. Feel the difference it makes. It might be easy to read without the pointer at 30 and 40 BPM, but the pointer might give you invaluable support while reading at 50 and 60 BPM. Observe how you feel and keep using the pointer to achieve your best performance. This is the big transition but be aware that even I use the pointer from time to time. Because each book requires a slightly different speed to read, I can get to the best pace to get the most out of it if I use the pointer. Sometimes I'm a little tired at the end of the day and I use the pointer when I start reading new material to help me to focus and perform to the best of my ability.

Go to the webpage below and start practising. Do it now!

www.thespeedreadingcoach.com/audio

4.2 The 10% strategy

I know that a new skill like speed reading is something that you will be developing over your lifetime, so I have a great piece of advice to help you improve further.

If you feel that you are not reading fast enough, there is a simple way to keep improving.

As you find yourself reading at a comfortable speed, use the 10% strategy. Always read the first paragraph of a chapter or article at your normal speed and then push to read 10% faster on the next paragraph. Then read the following paragraph at your normal speed again, if you feel the need to slow down. After that, push again to read 10% faster and you will be developing incrementally without noticing. Have you ever heard of compounding investment strategy? It works in the same way. You push just a little every other paragraph and the final development will be much bigger than you could have ever imagined.

This is the 10% strategy. Use it and your comfort zone will keep improving without much effort. Just push to go 10% faster from time to time and you will be developing yourself with or without the pointer.

Read in bursts

To help you focus your attention I suggest you try reading in bursts. Read faster until you reach a coma, period or any other punctuation sign. Because you make a micro pause after every burst you might notice the difference in relevance between different passages. It's like swallowing little bites of information that might contain interesting content or not. This is a simple and effective way to increase your reading speed and focus.

4.3 Calculating the time to read a whole book. Surprise, surprise!

Now for the best part of this book.

Do you remember that I promised that you would look at a book like you look at a DVD?

Let's say you want to choose a DVD to watch. Firstly, you are attracted by the picture on the cover; you then read the title, small description at the front and big description at the back; which is essentially what someone would do if they were selecting a book to read. The big difference is that the DVD has a number on the back cover that states the time it takes to watch the whole movie – and the book doesn't. In a general sense people will avoid starting a task if they have no idea about the time it will take to finish it. Therefore, I will show you how to work out the time to read any book of your choice. You will be surprised with the results.

Now, let's say you decide to read a book of 240 pages. How long will it take you to read the book? Well, this book has 240 pages.

Firstly, flick through the pages and notice how many empty pages you will find in the book. Some books leave a lot of dead space between chapters, or they are full of pictures and graphs. If that's the case, just have an approximate guess of how many pages you have as real text to calculate the time to read the book.

Assuming that the book you are reading right now has many pages lacking content at the beginning, some blank space between chapters and also pictures and graphs, I will estimate that 45 pages are basically empty of content – so I will delete them from the total.

To find out the time to read this book, I will round the numbers down to make it even easier.

Just multiply the number of words you have on one line by the number of lines you have on one page.

My book has 10 words per line and 25 lines per page, so I multiply 10 x 25 = 250 words per page. Now multiply 250 by the number of pages with text in the book. My book has 195 pages of real text. Therefore, 250 x 195 = 48,000.

This means that we have about 48,000 words in the whole book. I was rounding it down because there are lots of lines in the book that don't have 10 words per line and quite a few empty spaces.

Now just divide the 48,000 by your reading speed.
If you are reading at 300 WPM, you will take 160 minutes or two hours and 40 minutes to finish the book.

Reading at 400 WPM, you will take two hours. Reading at 500 WPM it will be only one hour and 36 minutes. Now at 600 WPM it's only one hour and 20 minutes, while if you are reading at 1000 WPM, you will take less than 48 minutes to finish the book. Isn't it incredible?

I would recommend that you take longer than that to read the entire book. Give yourself an additional 30 minutes as you will be stopping to mark the book, make notes, while reflecting on some of the main points. However, the actual time to read the book has been reduced because you now know how to speed read effectively.

Congratulations!

4.4 Saving time table and ROI

To have a quick overview of how much time you will be saving every day as a result of your improvement, please take a look at the table on the next page:

Time saved by improving your reading speed by 33%			
Reading hours per day (5 days a week)	Time saved per week	Time saved per month	Time saved per year
1 hour	1 hour 14 min	5 hours 20 min	8 working days
2 hours	2 hours 28 min	10 hours 41 min	16 working days
3 hours	3 hours 42 min	16 hours 2 min	24 working days
4 hours	4 hours 56 min	21 hours 22 min	32 working days

I've used 33% improvement as an example of your future average reading speed but I believe that after reading the book you might even have an overall improvement higher than 33%. Most of my clients can read 100% faster at times but they don't necessarily read 100% faster all the time.

If you read for work for on average three hours a day and have an average improvement of 33%, you will have an extra month of work every year. If you have employees, they will work one extra month for *free* every single year. I think this is a great *return on investment* (ROI) and you will hardly notice that you are reading faster because it will become second nature to you!

4.5 You are limitless

I will end this chapter with some wise words from Krishnamurti:

"The mind is so powerful that it can create an experience to support any belief. Then we believe the experience proves the belief, not knowing that the belief created the experience."

I believe that you can expand your knowledge by believing in yourself and daring to do things you have never done before.

Now, how long has it been since you did something for the first time?

You brain works as a whole organism. I believe that if you learn something new, your brain gets motivated to learn even more, which will reflect on your reading performance too. So, how about taking up a new hobby?

There is a field of knowledge called thematic interconnectedness that explains how we can learn from unusual sources. If you start learning how to dance you will feel challenged, but it is really refreshing to think with a beginners mind and see things anew. It can have profound effects on your life, and you can learn valuable lessons that can be applied to activities that didn't seem to have anything in common on the surface.

So, what about learning how to meditate and open the doors of perception?

There are many ways to get a taste for it. You can try either silent or active meditation. You can see the effects of meditation on your brain by watching biofeedback software mapping your brainwaves in real-time, or you can listen to frequencies that will make your brain vibrate in a new way, and you will be meditating like expert yogis in no time at all. There is also the 10-minute guided meditation that has been used by over 5 million people to date.

If you want to explore the secrets of your mind, you can visit the webpage below, and choose the right meditation technique to suit you.

www.thespeedreadingcoach.com/meditation

If you think meditation is too serious, and you just want to have some fun, why don't you try some cookery or music lessons?

You could even join a book club. Information is about timing, too. Certain books will attract serendipity; read more books and make your own luck.

Nothing is stopping you from becoming the perfect version of yourself. You are limitless.

Get out of the rut and create magic in your life.

Become a leading expert fast!

The *Think Shark System* will show you the five steps to help you become a leading expert fast. The steps are:

- **T** — **Target** a niche
- **H** — **How** to make three times as much money
- **I** — **Ignorance** is your best friend
- **N** — **Non-fiction** book written by you
- **K** — **Know** and share

To illustrate the process, I will compare the journey of finding your strategy to position yourself as an expert in your field to the body of a shark. Once you understand the links between the steps, you will be ready to start your journey and stay motivated until you achieve your expert status.

1 - Target a niche

Sharks are fascinating creatures that have been around since the dawn of time. They have an incredible sense of smell that gives them remarkable abilities of orientation, no matter if it is day or night. They can smell blood from three miles away.

As they lock the direction they have to travel to reach their goal in their mind, they use their tail as the main source of trust to reach their target. I use the tail analogy to represent targeting a niche.

This first step will help you become an expert by improving your metaphorical sense of smell and your propulsion power.

Once you are clear on why you chose your line of work, you will become not only inspired to serve, but you will inspire others to follow you. This is certain to propel your career forward and help make you stand out from the crowd as an expert.

2 - How to make three times as much money

The shark's dorsal fin is famous. It represents alignment, so just by seeing their fin above the waterline, you know which way the shark is going.

If you want to become more aligned with your purpose in life, you will have to start dropping inconsistent habits and attitudes.

This step will help you become inspired to pursue the incredibly helpful habit of reading more business books.

"According to the U.S. Labor Department, business people who read at least seven business books per year earn over 230 percent more than people who read just one book per year." [1]

Many of us spend huge amounts of money, time and perseverance to take a degree and end up making more money as a result of acquiring targeted knowledge.

We are living in exponential times, and anything is possible. Rest assured that just reading books you can double, treble or even increase your income by a factor of ten.

How many books would you like to read every year?

3 - Ignorance is your best friend

The shark is constantly swimming, even while sleeping. Can you imagine being that restless?

Many people have a mind that never stops. They feel that they need constant stimulation, and keep jumping from one subject to the next. Their judgement and decision-making power can get fatigued, and they become less responsive to changes.

The shark's body represents your body of knowledge, and the focus in this step is your information diet.

If you are allowing the media and social media feed your mind with content that is depressing and pointless, you can make a stand and decide to experiment living a low information diet. [You will be less informed about unimportant news/events, and more informed about things that matter]. The benefit of being ignorant about the news [and your social media 'friends' latest sock purchase / latest holiday plans / ...] is that you will finally find the time to start reading books and watching videos that can help you progress in your career. I read a daily digest with ten headlines and only click on one or two to read the full small articles. This way I am up to date, but I also avoid distractions like following sports.

Another source of insight and intellectual nourishment is the daily practice of meditation. So, I urge you to boost your mental health by trying one of the many forms of meditation, or start exercising, pick up a hobby or just have more nourishing down time.

4 - Non-fiction book written by you

The shark's brain is responsible for coordinating all its bodily functions and interactions with the environment, so I would recommend you to integrate all your knowledge and position yourself as an authority by writing your book. The word 'authority' contains the word author.

This is not as challenging as you might think. There are many resources that can help you with the process of writing, and I have recommended some courses to help you accomplish writing a book in a matter of a few months. You can even write your book by recording yourself giving an interview and paying someone to transcribe and organise your ideas into chapters. You will be amazed by the sense of achievement that comes from having your name on the front cover of a book. Incredible opportunities appeared in my life just because I invested the time to write this book.

So, what will your book be about?

5 - Know and share

The last step focuses on the shark's mouth. After all, that's what makes them famous.

They have several layers of teeth that keep growing and replacing themselves, so they always have sharp teeth and stay a top predator.

As an expert, your mouth can also make you famous. You need to express yourself and your ideas in order to make an impact on other people's lives. Sharpening your communication skills is crucial.

I recommend professionals that can help you create the perfect pitch, speak from the stage with confidence, or record your ideas and sell them as e-Learning courses.

As you keep learning and teaching, you will improve your power of persuasion.

By having your book written, you will have a solid platform to speak from, and will be surprised with the media attention, and admiration from family, friends and peers.

BECOME A LEADING EXPERT FAST

"The most important investment you can make is in yourself."

Warren Buffett

Read on to expand your mind and create a vision for your future. Develop a strategy to progress in life at speed and leave a legacy.

Time to read this chapter

at 100 wpm	1 h 44 min
at 200 wpm	52 min
at 300 wpm	35 min
at 400 wpm	26 min
at 500 wpm	20 min
at 600 wpm	17 min
at 700 wpm	15 min
at 800 wpm	13 min
at 900 wpm	12 min
at 1000 wpm	10 min

PART 1

Target a niche

5.1.1 The never ending learning cycle

Bill Gates and Warren Buffett were giving an interview at the University of Nebraska, and were asked:

"What superpower would you like to have?"

Bill Gates answered first: *"Being able to read-super fast! Yeah! That would be nice!"*

Warren Buffett replied: *"Yeah, that would be huge! Well…Bill can read super-fast. I mean, he reads about three times as fast as me. I probably wasted 10 years reading slowly."*

Your education defines you and when you know how to do something that not many people are able to learn you have an edge. And, even if you can read much faster than before, you can always still develop further! The world is constantly changing, but are you keeping up with the times?

Learning is important at all ages and stages of life, but most people are proud of finishing a degree and do not take learning seriously afterwards. Many people read three or four books a year and think they are doing quite well.

How many books did you read in the last 12 months?

10X thinking

Google founder, Larry Page, believes that it is often easier to make something 10 times better than it is to make it 10 percent better.

To do that, you need to make the shift from traditional linear thinking to entrepreneurial, exponential thinking.

"10x thinking" implies that you are willing to think big, embrace change, and disrupt both yourself and the industry you work in.

10X yourself

So, how can you improve yourself 10 times?

By not focusing on your existing skills and assumptions, and not putting extra effort on top of an existing solution. Instead, explore new fields of knowledge, be open to creative concepts and solutions and have breakthrough ideas that will make a big change in your life and, crucially, position yourself as an expert in your field.

Can you imagine the impact of reading 30 to 50 books in your field? You could certainly become an international expert in your area of knowledge just by keeping up with new developments. What about being the source of future thinking?

According to David Cottrell, if you read one book a month you are in the top one percent of all non-fiction readers in the world. How hard can this be?

I think that you can accomplish anything if you have a vision, stay motivated and employ the right strategy.

5.1.2 The future of science and your role as a revolutionary

My intention with this book is not only to teach you to speed read, it goes beyond that, by questioning your default way of thinking.

I'm leading the *Reading Revolution* and I invite you to break the boundaries of traditional knowledge, to disrupt new industries, and create your own revolution, to help us move towards the future. Whatever your field of work, something must change and evolve. By changing, you will not please everyone, there always will be people that will hang on to the past and be opposed to your new ideas but this is part of the challenge of creating a new world. As Arthur Schopenhauer wisely said: "All truth passes through three stages: First, it is ridiculed; Second, it is violently opposed; Third, it is accepted as self-evident."

Many well-established theories will be replaced, and I hope that my insights in this book will contribute to the evolution of the way we read and learn. Please don't trust me on everything I say; I would rather have you questioning me, because this is the way to create the future. Think…

Now, I want to share something that has challenged my way of thinking in a big way. I hope it can also expand your way of seeing how to live longer and become healthier.

My plan is to live healthily, until I'm at least 205 years of age. My grandfather, called Cartaxo, was the Chancellor of one of the most prestigious Agriculture Universities in Brazil for 7 years. He was an eccentric scientist, who had an amazing impact on my life.

Since an early age, I've learnt about chemistry and alchemy with my grandfather. Alchemy includes the creation of the philosopher's stone, and the development of the elixir of life, amongst other goals. He proved to me, and many of his students and colleagues, that stable elements like Silicon (atomic number 14) can transmutate into Carbon (atomic

221

number 6) and Oxygen (atomic number 8) without releasing extra energy from splitting an atom into two. Conversely, the atomic bomb works on the principle of releasing an enormous amount of energy from splitting atoms.

The dream of many alchemists is to transform lead into gold and I believe that we will be able to create gold from other elements and disrupt the whole market. We already create artificial diamonds so, why not gold or platinum? I've developed my scientific mind and have become very curious about finding alternative ways to challenge the status quo. It was very interesting to be able to challenge my teachers with advanced theories that questioned their obsolete way of seeing the world. I'd learnt about my grandfather's controversial theories, and I ended up studying Agricultural Engineering at University.

My grandfather was in really good shape almost until he died, aged 102, so I know I've got good genes but I'm really concerned about the way degenerative diseases are becoming more frequent even though scientists are developing more treatments and drugs. We are catching fewer diseases and we are becoming ill from the inside out, i.e. diabetes, Aids, cancer, Alzheimer's, coronary diseases, allergies and many more illnesses that were not commonplace when my grandfather was young.

Medicine has developed enormously yet we are getting sicker; why is that? Is it the result of a sedentary lifestyle with too many ready meals, a lot of sugar and the dreaded stress?

Well, one of the theories about the development of chronic diseases that also explains why we age, is called *Free Radical Theory of Aging* (FRTA). According to this theory, our cells become damaged because they accumulate free radicals, causing aging. Free radicals are atoms with unpaired electrons, or in simple words, these atoms need more electrons to become stable. If you eat fruit, vegetables and nuts with high levels of antioxidants, you supply extra electrons to your body, and chances are that you will become healthier, and will not develop cancer or other chronic diseases.

Now comes a new theory that I find intriguing.

In the book called *Earthing*, the authors, Clinton Ober, Stephen Sinatra and Martin Zucker say that we can tap into an abundant source of electrons that are bio available, from just under our feet, and it costs nothing.

Their theory takes into account that the introduction of rubber and synthetic soles for our shoes changed our electrical stability. Rubber is insulating in the same way as wooden floors or carpet, so we lost the contact with the earth, that we used to have 50 years ago while using leather-soled shoes. Our electrical appliances are connected to the earth to avoid damage and we should do it with our bodies too. We are electrical beings and we generate electricity which can be measured, for example, by the electrocardiogram (ECG). By grounding ourselves we become electrically stable because the earth has abundant electrons that can be absorbed by the body if you earth yourself by walking barefoot, or touching a conductive material that is grounded.

This is a theory based on science, that is still controversial, and it states that by grounding yourself you will reduce inflammation in the body and boost your immune system.

If you are a health practitioner, or are concerned with your own longevity, you can visit their website for links to their book, videos and resources, that could help you become a healthier person, and perform better at work and in life.

www.groundology.com

Another person I've been learning from is a Dutch man called Wim Hof. He is revolutionising the way we boost our immune system, treat chronic diseases and also fight mental illnesses. He teaches simple breathing techniques that have been proven scientifically to affect our bodies in ways never seen before. If you are curious about it you can google his name and watch some videos of his endurance challenges. You can also visit his website for a free introduction to his method.

www.wimhofmethod.com

If you think that all this science is nonsense, that's fine, do your research and make your own decisions. Remember that you can start thinking about how to revolutionise your own field of work. How would you do what you do today in 10 years from now? What could you invent?

5.1.3 Read more and succeed faster

I understand that people make decisions in life in search of pleasure or to avoid pain.

If you want to read more, it could be because you want financial freedom to be able to travel the world. This is a motivational strategy that comes naturally to many people; especially entrepreneurs. They take that risk with the self-belief that the future will bring them a fortune.

Contrary to being motivated towards success, some people are motivated to avoid pain. For example, you might want to read more to catch up with your colleagues at your new job because you are afraid of being fired if you don't start contributing at meetings.

There is nothing wrong with either of the options above; however, be aware that some people might run faster by seeing the carrot on a stick while someone else might run even faster just by the thought of a whip.

What is it for you?

Do you work hard to buy a bigger house or do you work harder because you are afraid of not being able to pay the mortgage, which may result in the loss of your home?

I'm a bit dramatic here but this is the truth that lies behind our desire to get things done. You are either searching for pleasure or you want to avoid pain.

The difference between motivation and inspiration

Most people join a gym because they intend to get fit. However, once the novelty of the gym wears off, they may decide to hire a personal trainer to achieve their goals.

Someone else may choose to go running for an hour each morning to get fit.

For some, the idea of waking up an hour earlier each morning may be an arduous effort, while for others, they feel the inspiration to do so.

If you were to plan to run the marathon in six months from now, would you require someone to urge you on to go running? I don't think so because you create a big vision of crossing the finishing line and you stick to your training regime. If you decide to run for charity, the commitment is even bigger and this way you might start creating gravity around your dreams and inspire others to join you and start running too. This way you become more inspired.

This is the difference between motivation and inspiration. Motivation comes from the outside; inspiration comes from the inside. You can hire a coach to help you perform better at anything but you don't rely on them because you have a burning desire to succeed.

So, I want to help you get inspired, and one good reason for you to start reading more could be that you want to make more money. Would you like to make more money? Read on to find out how.

PART 2

How to make
three times as much money

5.2.1 Read seven business books a year

I found some interesting information in the book Tuesday Morning Coaching by David Cottrell [1], and I quote him again:

"According to the U.S. Labor Department, business people who read at least seven business books per year earn over 230 percent more than people who read just one book per year."

I've shown you this information on the video that was flashing words very quickly. Do you remember?

Now, if you read 15 pages of a business book a day, you will be reading two books of 225 pages every month. This is 24 books in one year!

What about that for a challenge?

Anything related to business would count here so, if you like watching programmes that show a selection of good advertising campaigns on TV, then maybe you would find it interesting to read a book or two about advertising. You will broaden your knowledge with new ideas and perhaps one day you will be having a chat with your boss and suddenly you say something inspirational and who knows where that might take you in the future.

Business coaches

It's worth considering that any successful sports person has a coach to help them maximise their performance; in the same way, I believe that a business coach will help you improve your game, and be able to recommend many inspirational books.

I had a few business coaches that challenged me to develop my potential as a visionary. I can see myself impacting the whole world with this book, my online courses and by training others to ignite people's passion for reading books.

Once I had crystallized my exciting vision, I had invaluable help to execute it from a business coach from ActionCOACH called Parag Prasad, who told me to read a thought-provoking book called *Eat That Frog* by Brian Tracy. Brian's book is so short that I read it for the first time whilst still in the bookshop. It was so good that I bought a few copies to give as gifts to clients and friends.

My other coach is JT Foxx and I'm having a lot of fun with him. He is obsessed with business success, and he has been inspiring me to constantly reinvent myself. JT Foxx is controversial and his energy is infectious, so I hope you also have the privilege of being coached by someone like him. He recommended to me a book by Ashlee Vance, about an incredible innovator called *Elon Musk*; it's worth checking out.

Start searching for your business coach by following the link below.

www.thespeedreadingcoach.com/businesscoach

So, you may be reading books on marketing and a friend informs you of their desire to open a shop. Having listened, you come forward with some clever promotional ideas, which make an instant impression. So much so that your friend offers you a partnership deal of 20% stake in the business. Partnerships like that happen all the time because knowledge is a valuable commodity.

Now let's say that you have a good job, and you live comfortably. If you read books about how to buy a house to rent or invest your money, you might stay in the same job, but you will start making money by investing wisely, which is a great way to become financially independent.

If you have an important business meeting with a professional that has written a book, or that mentions his favourite business book in his LinkedIn profile, can you imagine the impact you would make by reading the book before the meeting? Even if you don't read it from cover to cover, you will understand a lot about that person and by showing interest in them, you will be miles ahead of the competition.

PART 3

Ignorance is your best friend

5.3.1 Become a thought leader

Years ago I read a fantastic book called *The Field* by Lynne McTaggart. She talks about learning, storing information in our memory banks and also creating original ideas and content. The interesting twist here is that, based on scientific observation, she believes that we store memory outside our brains or in the "field" around us, which means "in the air". The brain is used to tune into our memory or into new ideas that can be downloaded from this immense field of knowledge that surrounds us. She points out that no one has ever proved that we store memory inside ourselves, we can only observe some parts of our brain lighting up while we think or remember but this would be just the activation or our receptor station.

I believe that if you know what makes you tick, the magic key will turn whenever you start reading more about the subject you are passionate about and you will access information that has been developed by other people because everything is stored in the "field".

While writing this book I had many moments of profound inspiration where new ideas or concepts just crystallised in my mind and I felt like downloading the information from a higher level of awareness. I've heard and read that many authors have the same feeling of downloading information while creating fiction or making new discoveries. The interesting phenomenon is that certain discoveries in science happen simultaneously in laboratories that are not connected and are placed in different countries. This synchronicity is the proof that some people find a way to access this immense field of knowledge and come up with similar findings in different parts of the world.

If you read from 30 to 50 books on a particular subject, you can become an international expert in that area of knowledge. It is like taking another degree by yourself. If you read one book a week, you would read 52 books in a year and change your life.

Now take a look at these reading statistics from The Jenkins Group in the USA and get excited about reading a few extra books. You might get very inspired to read more and in doing so, awaken your hidden potential that will give you creative solutions to your challenges.

•   33% of high school graduates never read another book for the rest of their lives.

•   42% of college graduates never read another book after college.

•   80% of US families did not buy or read a book last year.

•   70% of US adults have not been in a bookstore in the last five years.

•   57% of new books are not read to completion.

Aren't these numbers incredible? Just make an effort to read a little bit more. When you apply this knowledge to your profession, you will be ahead of the masses that don't read and you will have the potential to generate more business and, ultimately, make more money!

Cultivate selective ignorance

It is interesting to note that we end up reading a lot of news and information that wastes time. I read a book called *The 4-Hour Work Week* by Tim Ferriss and he talks about cultivating selective ignorance. I think it is a brilliant concept that helps people to become more focused on subjects they want to learn and stop overloading themselves with trivia, social media and the news. If I read the paper, I am totally aware that I want to find news that can propel my business forward. I want articles with good random ideas or that have a direct connection with what I do, so that I can have new ideas or perhaps I will reach out and contact the journalist.

I glance through the paper and only stop when I find something that I really want to read. Similarly, I am ruthless about not opening emails just because they have a catchy subject line. Most of the time, I keep up-to-date by reading the *Yahoo! News Digest* App. They select 9 to 11 of what they consider to be the most important headlines of the day, and I click on them if they really grab my attention and interest. Another great source of news is Apple's *News* App. You select the sources you prefer and the more you read, the more personalised your News becomes. As I have already mentioned, I avoid watching the news on TV and, in this way, I create between 30-60 minutes in my day that I can then use to read a book and learn something that can really have an impact on my life.

Avoid decision fatigue

Yes, it is exciting to read the news and trivia on Twitter and Facebook. You release dopamine in your blood stream and you get turned on, but by forcing your brain to decide to read or ignore every single entry, you will get fatigued very quickly, and you will have less energy to focus on things that really matter. This is called *Decision Fatigue*.

My advice is to make fewer decisions and become more pro-active. Did you know that Facebook founder Mark Zuckerberg wears the same clothes to work every single day? Yes, grey T-shirt and a darker grey hoodie. His wardrobe has lots of the same pieces. He thinks that we can only make a limited amount of assertive decisions a day and he doesn't want to waste this power by having to decide which clothes to wear every single day, not to mention the decisions required while buying clothes. He is saving his decision power for things that are really important to him. Does it make sense or not?

Find your mission in life. Focus on just a few things that you care about every day of the week, and say NO to everything else that doesn't help you fulfil your dreams.

If you must check your Facebook and Twitter, limit the time spent to 10-20 minutes a day because this is usually a reactive activity. Do not let them hijack your life, instead find a meditation course or search on YouTube for a free lesson and learn how to focus your mind. I practice meditation to develop clarity and to fine-tune my purpose.

The idea is to start reading and researching about things that you like doing or about which you wish you had more information. Do not be restricted to reading books; browse the internet, follow people you admire, have a RSS Feed Reader, read book summaries, watch videos, listen to podcasts and audio programmes or talk to people about areas you want to develop.

What would you like to know more about?

If you like drinking wine, you could start by reading a book about a famous wine maker and understand a little bit about wines. It is inevitable that you will end up having new, stimulating things to talk about whenever you sit down with your friends around a good bottle of wine.

Why not learn about meditation, football or psychology? The choice is yours and I believe that by reading more you will expand your world and more opportunities will present themselves.

It is not by chance that many wealthy people have lots of books in their houses. Do you think that because they are rich, they find the time to read more books or because they find the time to read more books they end up becoming richer?

Whatever the case, reading simply brings you more knowledge and knowing more is fundamental in this changing world. Read a bit more and decide what you want to learn next. Ask your friends for recommendations and make a list of books you want to read. The possibilities are endless.

5.3.2 Find your limiting beliefs about reading

To improve your reading speed, it is important that you read more. I know that you have lots to read at work but you will need to choose a few books to start practising the principles I've introduced you to throughout the book. So, I would like to know what is your reason for not reading more than you are reading at the moment? This is a very important question, because just by identifying what is stopping you reading books, you will become aware of your limiting beliefs and therefore, you will get over some of them and start to develop your love for reading.

Please tick below all the reasons or excuses for not reading more books than you are actually reading. You might find many of them relevant to you; write down your private thoughts or reasons that are hindering your overall development. It is crucial to know why you don't read because I want to inspire you to read more and this is the first step. It will only take a minute to think about it.

Now tick all the reasons for not reading more books.

☐ I watch TV/movies instead
☐ I work late
☐ I'm already studying
☐ I go out to socialise
☐ I play video games
☐ I have a drink

- ☐ I'm too tired
- ☐ I think reading is a boring and slow activity
- ☐ I lack focus
- ☐ I have children to look after
- ☐ I'm not motivated
- ☐ It is not part of my routine
- ☐ I feel guilty about spending time reading instead of doing high priority things
- ☐ I like to spend time with my family

Add your own reasons or excuses below:

_____

_____

_____

_____

OK, now I want to ask you a critical question that might shake your limiting beliefs. Please read again all your reasons for not reading books and ask yourself after each reason. Is it true? Is it really true?

We always want to be right and to be so, we justify our actions with a few untrue ideas. I do it too!

I believe that it is with the best of intentions that you might think that you don't read more books because you work late or because you like to go out for a drink and socialise. But now thinking carefully, is it the real reason for not reading more? I would suggest otherwise. You could always find the time to read 15 pages of a book every day if you were really inspired to do so; excuses are just justifications, not true reasons.

I overcame some of my limiting beliefs by walking over hot coals with Tony Robbins. If you can do that you can pretty much do anything else.

Follow the link below to know more about this event.

www.thespeedreadingcoach.com/tony

5.3.3 Being addicted to TV can slow down your brain power

On average, people watch three hours of television a day. Some, however, can waste their life sitting in front of the TV.

I see it as an addiction like smoking or drinking. If you have a habit that is making you waste time it is possible that you are addicted to it and don't know how to break the habit. Perhaps you want to feel free to choose other alternatives to have fun, enjoy your free time or find new ways to become more productive and progress in your profession much faster. So, let's see if I can motivate you to read more and stop watching so much TV.

If you want real information, you need to read. Reading is a much faster way to gain knowledge than the TV and it brings much more content.

I believe that you could learn 10 times more reading the newspaper for 30 minutes than watching the news on TV. To me, it seems that the newsreader is just reading headlines from a newspaper and making superficial comments about them. The worst thing is that you can't even choose what you want to know, they just throw information at you that is seldom relevant in your life. I would recommend that you spend time choosing what you want to watch. Be careful not to watch just anything, just because you can't be bothered to switch the TV off. Make an extra effort to switch it off and you will have more time to live.

By the way, I've been living in London for 15 years and I didn't have a TV for at least 6 of those years because I feel happier this way. Could you get rid of yours? You could do an experiment and leave your TV at your friend's house for a month to decide if you really need it or not.

You can find the news on the internet and use filters and alerts to be notified about specific subjects in text or video format. Follow the thought leaders in your field and be ahead of the masses.

PART 4

Non-fiction book
written by you

5.4.1 Capture your dream

By developing your reading speed, you will be able to read two books a month by reading 15 pages per day. That is it.

Which subject or subjects would you like to become an expert in?

Sometimes it is painful to decide to change direction drastically but I guess I've learnt to make important decisions out of the need for leading an inspiring life.

Now I invite you to take a deep breath and try to guess some answers to these questions by filling the blank. Just exercise your mind by finding new possibilities for your life. Enjoy!

I want to learn how to _____

I want to study _____

I want to be better at _____

I want to understand _____

What would you like to learn more about? This could be the first step to developing a new hobby or a new way to have fun or make money. Please spend a minute or two thinking about the areas you would like to develop your knowledge in, write it down, research on the internet the best books for you and buy them. Do it now!

If you took some action, I invite you to look into the unknown and fly five years into the future. Are you doing anything different other than your day-to-day job? By starting to read more, you will enhance your knowledge and broaden your horizons. Just for fun, what would you like to be an international expert in?

I would like to be an international expert in

_____

I hope I got you thinking about that big dream that you want to make real. Keep thinking about it and be very specific because it will help you get started and find the books and people you want to learn from. This way you will attract your dreams. Open your eyes to the possibilities.

Create a Goal Map

As you are aware that your mind thinks in pictures, I want to share with you a great way to stay connected to your dreams and take action to get there. You've probably seen, or perhaps you've created, a vision board to focus your attention on things that you want to create in the future. I had vision boards before but they lacked structure. To combine left and right side of the brain, I use the Goal Map format, which is a creation of Brian Mayne. It puts your conscious and unconscious mind to work for you. Below is a representation of it and you can use pictures instead of drawings.

The structure is basically having a main goal at the centre and a few sub-goals on both sides of it. Then think WHY you want those goals and draw on the top of the Map and you will have the "Emotional Drivers" defined. The ladder creates the WHEN by defining a timeline. The HOW are the actions you need to take and they go on the right side of the ladder. Then you finish it by deciding WHO will help you achieve those goals and write the names of people or organisations that will support you on the left side of the ladder. That's it; you've spent time creating your future and now you can have it as a screen saver or hang it somewhere to remind you of your big dreams and the road map, which will take you to them.

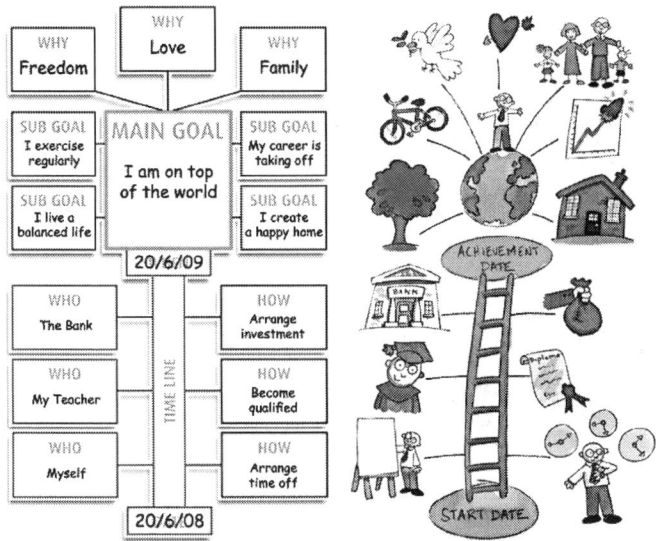

You can learn how to create your own Goal Map for free; use the easy to follow templates, or use the free online tool.

Go to the website below and you will find both ways to create your Goal Map.

www.goalmappingonline.com

I hope you enjoy it as much as I do!

5.4.2 Getting inspired

Another good question is: What would be a real reason for you to read more?

If you say that it is to have more knowledge, then the answer is good, yet there is no strength in it. You need to be more specific.

Please select the appropriate answers and then elaborate a little on them so you will have a clearer vision about the good reasons for reading more. Anything is possible once you are committed to a big vision.

If you would you like to have your own business, which business would it be? What could you do to get things started?

_____
_____
_____

Would you like to get a promotion at work? What would you like to do at the company you work at?

_____
_____
_____

Would you like to show off your knowledge while with friends? What would you like to be able to talk about?

_____
_____
_____

If you could choose where to work where would it be? Which country would you like to be living in?

_____
_____
_____

Would you like to have fun reading? Would you like to read some comedies, famous plays or classic literature?

_____
_____
_____

Would you like to make more money? How much are you planning to make and by when? If you are specific, chances are that you can achieve your target in less time. Start dreaming and planning now!

_____
_____
_____

I believe that if the reason is good enough, you will start buying and reading those books that support that dream; having a dream motivates us to accomplish incredible feats in life. Have you ever heard of Simon Sinek? He wrote a book called *Start With Why* and I think the book is fantastic. Google him and watch his talk on www.ted.com to get really inspired.

Please stop for a minute and think about the main reasons to read more. Jot them down and identify yourself with that feeling of accomplishment. This is just the beginning of an amazing adventure.

5.4.3 Become an author

Read more, capture the essence of the text and make notes. This way you will be actively remembering the information and will be able to play with it whenever you need.

I will be repeating myself here by suggesting that you could start your own blog. It will help you build your confidence and raise your profile on the internet. If you already have many blogs posted, then perhaps you can compile the information and write a book.

It started with a dream

The first time I thought I would be able to write a book was at a very inspiring presentation by Gerry Robert. He planted a seed inside my brain. This seed grew for five years, and now I have my book ready. The most surprising thing was to go to a seminar for entrepreneurs in London and meet him again after all those years. The timing was perfect and, with the book proof in hand, I enrolled on his course and got to learn the final steps to make the most out of publishing my book. He has a wonderful method of helping you write your book in a matter of months, not years. If you want to get your book done fast, follow the link below, attend one of his talks and enrol on his course. I regret not taking the plunge years ago; it would have saved me a lot of time and heartache. You will never be the same after listening to him.

www.thespeedreadingcoach.com/writeabook

I was involved with an incubator programme called *Key Person of Influence* and I don't think I would have succeeded writing such a transformational book without their guidance and support. I strongly recommend their programme if you are serious about making a dent in the universe. They helped me to position myself as an expert by creating valuable content and knowing how to share my knowledge in a way that is impactful and profitable. You can do the same. Check the link below to understand why they can help you too.

www.thespeedreadingcoach.com/keyperson

Now, I will share some practical ways to put your ideas into words.

If you prefer handwriting instead of typing, I discovered a pen that you can use to write as normal on a piece of paper and then the words are sent to your computer as text to be edited. Really fantastic if you keep writing notes on paper and want them organised on your computer. It also captures any drawing with accuracy. To find out more about it visit their website:

www.e-pens.com/uk

If you read a great passage from a book or document and decide to copy it for later editing, you can take a picture of it using a fantastic App called TextGrabber, and the text becomes editable.

Speed writing

I strongly advise you to learn how to touch type because this way you will stop the imaginary voice that sounds the words inside your head, which will create more flow to your thoughts.

It is interesting to notice that, by learning how to touch type, your body will start learning how to spell correctly; this is called muscle memory and it will guide your fingers to spell correctly without you having to think about the right spelling. Most people rely only on their visual memory to recall the right spelling and this might come as a surprise to most of you.

A web-based company called Read and Spell helps anyone to touch type including people with dyslexia and other learning difficulties. To learn more visit their website:

www.readandspell.com

You can also start to practise dictating your own book. There is an amazing App called *Dragon* that types whatever you are saying; just search for *Dragon* dictation. If you don't like dictating or the software makes too many mistakes, you can Google "transcription" and you will find a lot of people on Fiverr, PeoplePerHour or Upwork amongst other sites that will charge you very little to have it all typed up. You can record a lesson, conversation or talk you might give. You will start using the content you have in a written format without much effort.

Whatever your field I would say that even a small printed book will give you an enormous sense of satisfaction and it will help you position yourself as an expert in your area.

You can also re-purpose previous work and transform it into a book or eBook. You can always find extra help if you ask your friends, colleagues or search for professionals at Upwork.

www.upwork.com

I hope you find these tips inspiring and I hope that you decide to get serious about leaving a legacy in the form of a book. If you need help, please get in touch and I can recommend some professionals to help you structure your thoughts.

And if you write a book someday do let me know, I would like to celebrate this incredible achievement with you!

PART 5

Know and share

5.5.1 Relax with a book

A lot of people think of reading as a serious task and I believe it is useful to try new approaches to make the act of reading a more enjoyable activity.

Why don't you try to combine your leisure with reading?

I have a few suggestions:

Why don't you choose a good book and try to read it in the bath, pub, park or at the coffee shop?

If you like exercising perhaps you can go to the gym and try the bicycle or cross trainer and read your Kindle or iPad at the same time. If you prefer to run or cycle, you could try an audio book.

Instead of going out for a drink with a friend, why don't you have a glass of wine while reading a great book? By the way, I think that one glass is usually enough to keep my mind alert. After that, you are at your own peril.

I think this is a good way to be more relaxed while reading and to feel more confident to speed read and grasp the meaning of the text with less effort. Have a go and see if you like it! Make sure you are older than the age limit in your country to be able to drink!

Why don't you read out loud to your friend or partner? Children like to be read to and adults love it in the same way! People stop reading beautifully written or interesting books to us just because we know how to read. I don't think it makes any sense. So, why don't you grab a book of your choice and read for a person you love? You will have food for thought and good reasons to think about different things. I like to read about subjects that the other person would choose themselves. Select chapters that they might like from a psychology or history book. Be clever with your choices and you will have great fun reading to each other.

5.5.2 Creating a strategy to accomplish anything

To make the most of what you have learnt, I invite you to take the *Read Three Books In Three Weeks Challenge*. This way you will start a habit that can last a lifetime.

Read Three Books In Three Weeks Challenge

By now you know that a 200-page book might take you approximately two or three hours to read. So if you stop watching the news, and start reading 30 pages a day, you will be on target to read one whole book a week.

You will see how easy it is, if you plan it in advance.

This is the strategy to read one book a week:

Start with books with less than 200 pages. Divide the number of pages of your book by seven, to know how many pages to read per day. Use 7 post-its to mark the targets for each day. To estimate how much time you will read each day, measure your reading speed. Calculate the time to read each day. I am sure it will be less than you think. 30 minutes a day could well be enough.

Now decide which TV programme you will not watch (what about not watching the news?) or what other activity you will avoid, to create time for reading your book. Decide what time you will start reading each day, and stick to it.

To stay focused, skip any paragraph or chapter that you are not really interested about.

Jot down the big ideas from the book, and decide how to apply them to your work or life.

The key is to have an exciting list of books to read and have a routine for reading your books. It could be when you commute to work, or alternatively, once a week you decide not to watch another movie and use the time to read a good book instead.

The almost foolproof way to achieve any goal

If you need a helping hand, check this out! There is a free web-based service called www.stickk.com that can help you achieve your goals because you will use a *Commitment Contract*. You can also use the App *StickK* after registering on their website. You will define your goal (read three books in three weeks, lose 20 pounds, quit smoking or whatever you decide), pick a timeline to accomplish it, and put something at stake (whether it is money or your reputation). You are up to three times more likely to achieve a goal if you put money on the line. *StickK* allows you to bet on yourself and, if you are unsuccessful in achieving your goal, they will donate your money to charity, a friend, or even an organisation you oppose. For extra accountability, you can ask a friend to be your referee. You can also invite your friends to be your supporters, and they will automatically receive weekly updates on your progress.

After defining your goal on *StickK,* you can set up daily reminders at a certain time of the day so you will stay on track. For that, I use the App *Habit Builder* because it shows graphs of my progress with different metrics. It is great to be able to see my progress, visually, over a week or a month.

I would suggest that you choose books with less than 200 pages for the *Read Three Books In Three Weeks Challenge* to maximize your chances of successfully accomplishing your goal.

If you want to help inspire people to read more books, you can donate to the charity I support, *The Reading Agency.* If you choose to donate your money to a charity on the www.stickk.com website, they will donate your money to a charity of their choice. To donate to *The Reading Agency,* please choose to donate to a friend and search for me as the *Recipient of your Stakes.* My username is "alexgarcez" or email "alex@thespeedreadingcoach.com". I will donate all the money sent to my *StickK* account to *The Reading Agency* charity. Learn more about this amazing charity by going to the following webpage:

www.thespeedreadingcoach.com/donate

5.5.3 Creating your book list

To start the challenge, you need to create your book list. If you already have some titles written down, compile all the books in one Excel spreadsheet. This will help you to get organised and start the process of keeping track of your development. You can also rate the titles and summarise the important points from the books.

To help you select the books for your reading list, you can search the web for lists of the best, or most recommended, books in your field. You can ask your friends for their recommendations, but the best people to go to are your boss, people you admire in your organisation or some of your best clients. Tell them you have learnt how to speed read, and ask them if you can borrow some of their books. If they agree, borrow one book at the time, and give yourself a time limit to give it back. This way you will be more motivated to start and finish the book, and your friend/boss/client will not be worried that you will keep the book forever. If you have promised to give the book back within two weeks and you do not finish reading it on time, call them and ask for an extension of a week to finish it. Keep your word and return the book before the due date. This way you will start understanding how they think, you will have informed conversations, and it is very possible that you will be promoted sooner than expected.

Ethical cheating

If your list becomes too long and you want to get through it faster, you can start reading book summaries too.

Some people might think that reading a summary would be akin to cheating, but I think otherwise.

By reading the summary, you can identify the key messages of the book and learn precious concepts in a fraction of the time and, in addition, you can use it to increase your reading speed.

If you read the summary and conclude the new information learnt was sufficient, you can start reading another summary. However, if you think of the summary as a trailer for the book or a preview, you will spend 5-10 minutes evaluating if you really want to read the book or not. If you decide to read the book after reading the summary, you will be able to read your book faster and avoid skipping back to re-read because you have already found the key messages. Therefore, you will not be afraid of missing anything out and will be more confident reading the book at a faster pace.

I have selected some sources for book summaries for you to choose from. Some of them you pay for, and some are totally free of charge. Some of them are in convenient text, audio and video formats. There is also a website called *Read It For Me* that provides well-produced, 10-15 minute videos that summarise the books in a memorable way. There are websites that specialise in summarising business books, personal growth books and biographies. There is also a website called *eNotes* that has study guides, literature criticism and also summaries of fiction and non-fiction books.

I have also selected many websites that can help you learn through video. For example, the TED talks have remarkable speakers that convey an idea in 18 minutes or less. Many of the speakers are also authors. In addition, there is the relatively less famous YouTube Education and the iTunes University.

To wrap it up, you can buy software that changes the playback speed of any video, and you can save valuable time by fast forwarding a video 2, 3 or 4 times, while still understanding the message.

Go to the website below to find the links to all the summaries, videos and resources.

www.thespeedreadingcoach.com/summaries

I understand that people have natural abilities in certain areas but sometimes we push ourselves too hard to learn things that are almost out of reach for us to stay in flow and develop. For this reason I would suggest you to read the next topic, it might help you develop your natural talents in an easy and surprising way.

Now think about this...

5.5.4 Wealth Dynamics profiling test can help you choose great books to read

There are many profiling systems on the market, and I have tried several of them, including the *Enneagram, Myers-Briggs, DISC* and *Spiral Dynamics*. However, best of all is the *Wealth Dynamics Profile* because it's not only about knowing more about yourself but also how to find your strength to work in flow. This way you can find the right people that can leverage your value in a mutually beneficial way.

The reason for mentioning it is because once I took the test, I could clearly see why some successful people share the same profile as I do and by reading their biographies and books, I became much more in tune with myself and also inspired to read more.

There is nothing better than reading about the kind of people we like the most. Ourselves!

Even if I choose to read a book that is not about my profile, I can appreciate it and I will know what to focus on, without having to worry.

I'm certain that you will find it fascinating. You will learn how to get into flow and will create much more wealth into your life.

It totally changed the way I see work and money, so go on, take a quick look at it.

You can find more information about the test on the following webpage.

www.thespeedreadingcoach.com/wealth-dynamics

5.5.5 Creating targets for the month with the *Mini Max Target*

I have explained to you how to use the *Mini Max Target* to set up your reading target for each day in Chapter 8. Do you remember how it works? Now, let us set some targets for the month.

I have a target of reading two books a month. If I read 15 pages a day (my daily target), I will read 225 pages in 15 days. I can read half a book or, at least, browse the book and read some parts that are of interest to me. I do not think I need to read the whole book on every occasion. I prefer to move on unless the book is one of those that compels me to read on. In this case, it is possible that I will create more time to read and finish the book sooner. If it is not that exciting, I read half of it and skip around to get the general idea and move on to another one, ever hopeful that it will be a great one!

I think it is much better to get as much as you can from a book in about a week, even if you skip parts of it because the content is fresh and condensed in your mind and you get a great overview of the book. You will have a more complete memory of it than reading it slowly and carefully for three months because by the time you get to the end you will have probably forgotten the beginning! Would you prefer to watch a movie in one sitting, even if you have a few distractions along the way, than watch a movie in 10 sittings throughout three months? Books work in the same way.

So, my *Target* per month is to read two books. But my *Mini Target* is one book a month, and the *Max Target* is four books a month.

By the way, you can adapt the *Mini Max Target* to other activities you want to introduce into your routine, like exercise, organising your house, learning a language or anything else you might think of!

If you feel like you don't have enough time in your day to accomplish your targets I suggest you read a book called *"The Miracle Morning"* by Hal Elrod. He might be able to help you understand how to wake up a little earlier to create more quality time in your day.

www.miraclemorning.com

5.5.6 You can remember more of what you read if you have a big why

We learn something and start to forget about it very quickly. Most people believe that it is difficult to remember information from a book but, in fact, we also forget things we say very quickly. If you have a chat for two hours with a friend and try to remember what you've talked about, you would say that you remember just a few subjects of the conversation. But as you start to talk about it, you start to remember more.

We are very hard on ourselves when we think about comprehension from books or text; in spite of that, I believe that you will comprehend and remember more of what is higher up in your list of values.

I did a bit of acting while at University, and I remember that while rehearsing for a role, I had to feel like the character I was playing while having to memorise a lot of text. I had a buddy to help me to go through the lines – but it was tough. Nowadays, a lot of people want to become actors and get famous, but the question is, do they have what it takes? Do they have a good memory to remember all those lines with great detail?

Now a question for you:

Do you think that actors who succeed get ahead because they already had a good memory?

I don't think this is true. I believe that if they really want to succeed, they will develop a good memory. Be aware that they might be great at memorising lines; however, they will forget their partner's birthday or forget to put the rubbish out when it is collection day.

I think that good memory is all down to values. You always have time, money, focus and a good memory for whatever you value the most. The hard thing is to find out what you really like from your own heart and not by trying to copy other successful people. You can emulate other people but you need to develop your own authenticity to support your personal growth.

In the same way, do doctors have a good memory?

Not necessarily; they will develop good memory because if they get confused about the name of a drug to prescribe to a patient instead of curing them, they can kill them. This is enough reason to see medication as high value and therefore, they will remember all those confusing names of drugs. If you can remember this example, you will be able to help yourself to find out what really inspires you.

Whenever you understand what makes you tick, you will find more reasons to support your learning and you will develop your memory automatically.

I wish I could understand what singers are saying when they sing. Most of them are very hard to understand. I like the music and I can cope with not understanding the message because I'm not a singer. If I were, I would search on the internet for the lyrics. I would read and memorise them to have a great understanding of the song. But I like dancing, so for me, it is enough to listen to the music and shake my bones.

Decide what you want to focus on and more of it will start showing itself to you. Based on my own experience I can say that what you think about you bring about!

5.5.7 Share your knowledge to lead your field

By teaching, we really master our abilities and I would recommend that you help someone to read faster and give them the incentive to read more. Just help them using a pointer and they will thank you for that.

Why don't you start writing a blog with some of the good ideas you've been having or quotations from books you read? Make comments on other people's blogs, posts or randomly find people on the internet to talk about things you like in all those forums or chat rooms.

Once you become strong in your area of knowledge, you can start exchanging information and also start forming joint ventures to leverage your value through other people's connections.

A great place to share your ideas is called *"Toast Masters International"*, which is a great place to learn and practise public speaking. These are very supportive groups and they cost nothing if you want to visit a group and feel the atmosphere of excitement when people go on stage to share great information. If you decide to join a group, they will give you a lot of support and because they are a not for profit organisation, they cost around £100 pounds each year. There are other options on the market that might suit your needs better. If you are serious about building a career delivering content from the stage or by creating online courses, you can visit the webpage below to understand why I recommend Andy Harrington as one of the best professionals to help you structure your presentations and succeed in this profitable market.

www.thespeedreadingcoach.com/stage

Create a study group with friends or join a group and discuss any subject you are interested in. Visit the website below to get started.

www.meetup.com

5.5.8 Join or create a book club

If you join a book club, you will have the opportunity to have a peer group to help you discover a new world through books. The more you talk about books, then the more you learn from them. You learn how to structure your thoughts by having to give your opinion about a book or a subject. It helps you to gain greater confidence in discussing new subjects.

You can find real or virtual book clubs for business, science fiction, gay, short stories, Asian subjects or anything you can think of.

If you Google "Book Club" you can find a group to join and also make friends. If you don't find the book club you wanted just start one and in no time, more people will join you. We are living in incredible times and you can meet up over Skype too. Invite a friend to try it with you.

5.5.9 The next level

According to Albert Einstein, *"Wisdom is not a product of schooling but the lifelong attempt to acquire it."*

I shared, at the beginning of this book, that out of desperation I learnt how to cheat at school. Now I just do my best, because I believe that life is experimental and I learn a lesson every single day.

The future of learning

I'm leading innovation by launching the NewTycoon platform in the UK, which is a subsidiary of Success Resources, the biggest seminar promoter in the world.

I've also been invited by NewTycoon and Success Resources' CEO, Richard Tan, to coach thousands of people from their platform all over the globe. They already organise 500 events in 30 countries a year to promote great speakers, and with NewTycoon they are creating a global community, to help you learn how to succeed in this competitive world with practical knowledge that is not taught at school or university.

My first speaking engagement will be at an associate Success Resources' event for 2,000 people in Kazakhstan in November 2017, alongside 'The Wolf of Wall Street', Jordan Belfort. In the future I hope to have the privilege to share the stage with renowned people and I'm looking forward to speaking alongside presenters like Tony Robbins, Sir Richard Branson, Robert Kiyosaki, Larry King, Steve Forbes, Bill Clinton, Tony Blair, Rudy Giuliani, Les Brown, Jay Abraham, Eddie The Eagle and Baroness Mone of Mayfair.

In a bold move, Success Resources is revolutionising education using cutting edge technology and groundbreaking content, expanding their reach to 196 countries in 2017. Their seminars will become available through live streaming to your mobile phone if you become a NewTycoon member.

New stages will start popping up around the globe because they are partners with ARHT Media, the world's first complete end-to-end solution for the creation, delivery and monetisation of human holograms. They are already beaming presenters live for a two-way interaction with an audience.

And it doesn't stop there, because Tony Robbins, leading presenter at Success Resources' stages, is a partner with NextVR, the only platform that can deliver live events in virtual reality with the energy and the passion of a truly immersive experience.

FOX Sports, Live Nation, NBC Sports, HBO/Golden Boy and CNN have all partnered with NextVR and they are delivering one live event per week to 10 million people at the beginning of 2017. This number is expected to increase 10 fold by the end of the year and education is on the agenda for a dramatic and profound transformation. Tony is preparing new VR presentations to change your life and I'm creating a VR session that will blow your mind.

If you want to learn in full immersion and develop yourself at speed you need to learn about NewTycoon.

If you are a presenter and want to lead your field, you need to innovate and anticipate the new trends. Be the first one to offer new possibilities to your customers by understanding what the future holds.

If you join the NewTycoon community, you will also be able to make money just by telling your friends about the platform. Visit the webpage below to learn more about it:

www.thespeedreadingcoach.com/newtycoon

The books of the future

A little while back, I was talking to *Dragon's Den* UK star Simon Woodroffe OBE about the future of reading and learning. At the finish of our conversation he looked me in the eye and asked me a question:

"Can you create a book that can be automatically read faster?"

I smiled, and almost without hesitation said:

"Yes, I can."

He left, but the question remained with me. This was a massive challenge and many ideas floated inside my mind until I found the solution.

I'm happy to report that the books of the future are coming soon... I have created them, and I believe that you will love to automatically read faster.

Advanced techniques

Now, if you would like to improve even further, I can coach you how to use advanced strategies to find information faster so you can make decisions in half of the time with confidence. Please get in touch for information.

Email me on alex@thespeedreadingcoach.com

Keynote speaker

I am happy to book a flight to deliver a keynote speech at your organization, or to deliver a course to your team or your family anywhere in the world. Please get in touch for information.

Email me on alex@thespeedreadingcoach.com

Online course

If you prefer to learn how to speed read with a dynamic online course, you can learn it all while watching a video.

This is the link for the Basic + Advanced 4 hour online course.
www.udemy.com/speed-reading-for-business

The Practitioner course

Please get in touch if you want to take the Practitioner course and become a certified Speed Reading Coach. You will be able to help your family, friends and clients ignite their passion for reading books, while creating an extra source of income.

My mission is to help busy and ambitious professionals to gain knowledge faster and to develop peak performance with minimum effort in order to promote innovation in their company and in their life.

Give me your feedback

What is working for you? Please share with me your discoveries about how to be more efficient while reading and learning.

Email me on alex@thespeedreadingcoach.com

Or connect with me on Twitter, LinkedIn, my Facebook page or any other media. Visit my website to stay connected...

www.thespeedreadingcoach.com

I teach what I want to learn, and I like to say that:

"To read and not to share your ideas is not yet to learn. Action is necessary to hold information alive in your mind."

So share the love...

P.S. You can go back and read the introduction if you didn't read it yet.

FAIR EXCHANGE

In the event that you get more value from my book than the amount you have paid, I invite you to buy one or more copies of this book and give them as a gift to people you care about, so they will develop their passion for reading books and progress in their careers at speed.

You can also donate money to my cause, and help young people and adults who struggle with the written word or who don't read for pleasure.

Can you imagine not being able to read well?

One in six adults in the UK struggles to read and they find it difficult to develop themselves.

Did you know that reading for pleasure is more important to children's successes than education or social class?

I'm supporting The Reading Agency's initiative to make English pupils the most literate in Europe within five years. I share their enthusiasm, and I am dedicated to helping them achieve this goal faster.

You can do the same!

THE
READING
AGENCY

The Reading Agency inspires more people to read more, encourage them to share their enjoyment of reading and celebrate the difference that reading makes to all our lives. Because everything changes when we read.

Learn more and make a donation at:

www.thespeedreadingcoach.com/donate

I will be able to contribute more if you could support me by writing a short review about your achievements on Amazon, on the iBooks Store or on LinkedIn.

Thank you in advance for your help,

ACKNOWLEDGEMENTS

I'm fortunate to have met some fantastic people that definitely changed the direction of my life.

Special thanks to my wonderful mum Marly, Tuc Garcez, Gizela Quefaz Garcez, Miki Garcez, Otto Garcez, Cynthia Garcez Rabello, Ricardo Rabello, Rodrigo Garcez Rabello, Marina Garcez Rabello, Alcebiades Guarita Cartaxo, Carmen Pereira Cartaxo, Manuel Garcez, Miuda Garcez, Edgard Cotta, Betty Cotta, Fabio Cartaxo, Dulce Cartaxo de Souza, Silvio Modesto de Souza, Romilda Dessimoni Cartaxo, Eduardo Pereira Cartaxo Jr, Eithel Horta, Wanda Horta, Cid Horta, Alex Horta, Carolina Paiva Ferretti, Tevo Durães, Beleza Ferreira, Marcelo Pires, Alfredo Bufren, Aryon Lobo, Liss Barducco, Lizie, Carla Choma, Amaury Cortes, Sarita Paciornik, Lais Katz, Mini Boscardin, Conde, Ernani de Oliveira, João Candido Pereira de Castro Neto, Jamil Snege, Graciela Ines Presas Areu, Claudio Roth, Liss Barduco, Ana Paula Arosio, Nitzan Leon, Paul Bailey, Charlie Taillard, Sam Heath, Dan & Aurelie, Jim Cousins, Geoff Brownlow, Oliver Brownlow, Marcus Fumagalli, Sonia Maria Rinaldi, Caio Rinaldi, Mark Smith, Kathryn Lovewell, Liz Walker, Gal Stiglitz, Daniel Browne and my lovely friend Esther Helfen for inviting me to come to Europe and introducing me to the amazing Regis and Catherine Justome which I'm forever grateful for.

The business insights from Roger James Hamilton, creator of the Wealth Dynamics profiling system.

The love and trust from my eternal love Lollie Erb. You are a truly inspiring woman that opened my heart to love. You deserve the best in this world.

The support to develop a leading brand from the Key Person of Influence programme. Highlighting Daniel Priestley, Marcus Ubl, Darshana Ubl, Andrew Priestley and Tom Banjanin.

The inspiration to dream big came about from seven inspiring magicians that I had the opportunity to meet and learn from: Tony Robbins, Dr Richard Bandler, Paul McKenna, Chris Howard, Paul Dunn, Jonathan MacDonald and Dr John Demartini.

The support to be bold comes from my mentor Steve Bolton, founder of the successful franchise Platinum Property Partners.

Invaluable knowledge about social media came from Penny and Thomas Power. They are the founders of Ecademy, one of the first online networking communities to grow big, ages before Facebook and LinkedIn were on the map.

The support from Nili Raviv, creator of The Raviv Method, gave me the understanding and tools to get out of dyslexia.

The inspiration to start creating video products and reach out beyond my little world was from Darren Shirlaw, founder of Shirlaws Coaching.

Thanks to Mike Harris, creator of three iconic billion pound brands, for helping me communicate to the world what I do best in very simple words.

Invaluable criticism and excellent copy-editing of this book are from David Pilkington. Second copy-editing is from Kim Kimber.

Final touches under the supervision of my great friend Namita Kapila, founder of Interlanguage London, which is an English school for business and high-level students.

The cover design took shape after great criticism from Shaa Wasmund MBE and Matt Thomas, founders of Smarta, Digital Marketing expert Mark Attwood and Andy Coley, founder of Beyond Training Solutions.

The cover and back cover content would not be clear without insightful contribution from my friend Rebecca Redwood. She also suggested that I should explain the reason for choosing Arial type font for the book.

Last minute inspiration to write a compelling tagline from Master Theta Healing Practitioner and Instructor Anna Kitney. Final touches supervised by my friend Richard Cotton.

Understanding how to be a top keynote speaker from bestselling author Andy Harrington. Thanks to Andy Harrrington, Rima Aleksandraviclute, Marion Bevington and Jessen James for helping me write my story. Great feedback from my presentation from Mastanee Ati and Steve Talbot.

Insights into the publishing world from bestselling author Shaa Wasmund MBE, Mindy Gibbins-Klein at Panoma Press and Gerry Robert at Black Card Books. Their support and friendship were very important in finishing this book.

Inspiration to create the books of the future from Simon Woodroffe OBE.

Business development sprung from my business coaches from Action Coach, Parag Prasad and Shweta Jhajharia; Ian Christelow, master licensee of Action Coach in the UK and also Brad Sugars, founder of Action Coach.

Clarity to communicate my vision and mission from my friend Alistair Lobo. He is one of the most insightful business coaches I've ever met.

Help to contact the media and spread the news from business strategists Shaa Wasmund MBE and Matt Thomas.

Invaluable lessons about changing my internal reference points and contributing to a better world from my coach JT Foxx.

Profound inspiration to become a better communicator and expand my reach by building strong teams from Millionaire Mind Intensive presenter Mac Attram of Mindspace Associates.

I want to express my gratitude to Lydia Tan for shining her light on me and introducing me to Jennifer Cao, founder of NewTycoon, which lead me to meet Tony Robbins and eventually opened the doors of a portal to a new dimension where I met Success Resources' CEO Richard Tan and Veronica Chew, that invited me to become a speaker at their international platform and also one of the first NewTycoon Ambassadors in the world. Oliver Tham for the spiritual guidance, Vivien Leow and Ken Sapp for the business leadership, relentless support from Emileigh Tan, Casper Chen, Evon Lian, Debbie Dela Cruz and Alex Yeoh. Incredible videos created by talented media guru Ken Okazaki. Thank you to fellow Ambassadors, Krishna Gurung, Richard Wombwell, Harry Sardinas, Lily Patrascu, Hock Chong and my friend Annie Le for all support and inspiration to grow an idea into a thriving business for us all.

Special thanks to all my students, you keep inspiring me to become a better teacher and an eternal learner.

I feel indebted to the United Kingdom and I thank Her Majesty Queen Elizabeth the Second for inviting me to become a British Citizen. I will do whatever it takes to improve the quality of our education to standards never imagined before by helping everyone, from children to adults, develop their passion for learning and the UK will lead the way to a prosperous and peaceful world.

Finally, I thank God for blessing me with my life that hasn't been short of challenges. The adventure continues.

ABOUT THE AUTHOR

Alex Garcez gave up his Engineering degree in the third year because he was a very slow reader, however, his weakness became his strength when he took a speed reading course and decided to become an entrepreneur. He then took a Business Degree, Masters in Marketing and Advertising, and developed the *Revolution Speed Reading Method*. He has 13 years experience and he personally coached more than 3,600 people, including professionals from Goldman Sachs, J P Morgan, Google, GE, Bloomberg, eBay, The Wall Street Journal, The Walt Disney Company, KPMG, Ernst & Young, Home Office, Thomson Reuters, Adecco, Foreign and Commonwealth Office, Lloyds Bank, Citigroup, Sage, Bank of America, PwC, HSBC and O2.

Alex is leading the *Reading Revolution* because he discovered that your brain loves speed, and thinks that fast is fun - slow is boring - In fact, it gets bored and distracted if we read slowly and keep skipping back to reread.

He can help increase productivity at the office with such a smooth and simple methodology, that he guarantees that the participants will be able to read 50% faster in just four hours, or he will give them their money back. In fact, he is certain that most people can read 100% faster.

Alex is delivering a brand new service in the world called *Dine & Learn* with a challenge called *The Read 50% Faster Challenge*, to teach successful executives how to read faster, while having a meal & drink, at the *Hilton Canary Wharf Hotel* in London.

With more than 20,400 clients taking his online course in 135 countries, the average rating of the course is 4.5 stars our of 5, which means it works, even remotely.

With the introduction of training over Skype, Alex is challenging everyone in the world to unlock their potential. He is certain that the great majority will succeed! Professionals will become more focused to do their jobs, and also have more time to think creatively. Students will be able to advance in their fields at a greater speed.

Another reason for *The Read 50% Faster Challenge* is to promote the habit of reading books. This way we can boost the British economy to unprecedented levels.

He believes that everyone can fast forward their career, if they learn simple and powerful techniques that can boost confidence and assertiveness when making decisions in our fast-paced world.

His speed reading training is straightforward and clear. You will assess your reading speed at the beginning and throughout the book so you will be able to measure the Return on Investment (ROI) from the book. His approach to reading is holistic, by applying the tips, tools, techniques, software and shortcuts he helps each individual to perform at their personal best to become the leading expert in their field fast.

A NOTE ON THE FONT

Traditionally we find serif fonts in print, but according to bonfx.com which automatically tracks usage of the most popular web fonts across Alexa's top 10,000 sites, the most popular font in 2015 was Arial (20%) and Verdana (10%) which are both sans-serif fonts.

As we are increasingly reading on screens, I decided to use the sans-serif font Arial because you will be more likely to improve your reading speed if you are reading a familiar font than an obscure font.

I considered using the new font OpenDyslexic that was recently launched by Amazon on Kindle, that aims to help dyslexic people read easier, but I was swayed by the benefits of a familiar font.

After a lot of research, I found more evidence that my choice was justified:
• Arial and Times are read faster than Courier, Schoolbook, Georgia and all the other fonts. [2]

• Arial and Courier are considered the most legible fonts. [3]
• Arial was considered the most Youthful & Fun type and Times the least, from 12 popular fonts. Not

surprisingly Times appeared to be the most Business-like font. [3]

- Arial has been the most preferred font in studies that examined children, older adults, and college students. [3]

REFERENCE LIST

[1] David Cottrell, . (2013). Book title: Tuesday Morning Coaching - ISBN: 978-0-07-180615-2, MHID: 0-07-180615-6, or ISBN:978-0-07-180614-5, MHID: 0-07-180614-8

[2] Michael Bernard, Bonnie Lida, Shannon Riley, Telia Hackler, & Karen Janzen, . (2002). A Comparison of Popular Online Fonts: Which Size and Type is Best?. usabilitynews.org. Retrieved April 25, 2016, from <http://usabilitynews.org/a-comparison-of-popular-online-fonts-which-size-and-type-is-best/>

[3] Michael Bernard, Melissa Mills, Michelle Peterson, & Kelsey Storrer,. (2001). A Comparison of Popular Online Fonts: Which is Best and When?. usabilitynews.org. Retrieved April 25, 2016, from <http://usabilitynews.org/a-comparison-of-popular-online-fonts-which-is-best-and-when/>

24015479R00161

Printed in Great Britain
by Amazon